irish
POETRY
NOW

£4-50

irish
P O E T R Y
N O W

OTHER VOICES

Edited by Gabriel Fitzmaurice

WOLFHOUND PRESS

First published 1993 by
WOLFHOUND PRESS
68 Mountjoy Square
Dublin 1

Wolfhound Press receives financial assistance from the Arts Council/An
Chomhairle Ealaíon, Dublin, Ireland.

British Library Cataloguing in Publication Data

Irish Poetry Now: Other Voices
     I. Fitzmaurice, Gabriel
     821.91408

ISBN 0-86327-379-3

Typesetting: Wolfhound Press
Cover design: Valerie O'Dwyer
Cover illustration: Detail of illustration from *The Great Book of Ireland/
Leabhar Mór na hÉireann* by kind permission of the Trustees.
Printed by the Guernsey Press Co Ltd, Guernsey, Channel Isles.

CONTENTS

INTRODUCTION

For too long there has been consensus about the state of Irish poetry. Hierarchies have been established, *saoithe* elevated to positions that are as meaningless as they are irrelevant. What does it mean to be a poet in Ireland as we approach the twenty-first century? Poets have slipped considerably from being the unacknowledged legislators of the world — I doubt we ever were! But Dáibhí Ó Bruadair complained 'Mairg nach fuil 'na dhubhthuata' ('It's best to be a total boor'), such was the lack of appreciation for Gaelic poets and poetry in seventeenth-century Ireland; and today Mícheál Ó hAirtnéide (Michael Hartnett) asks 'Muna bhfuil gá le filíocht cén fáth go bhfuil filí ann?' ('If there's no need for poetry, why do poets exist?')

For me, poetry is about moments, insights. Poetry is all around us — it only remains for us to see it. Many see. The poet is the one who 'words' it. This is where much contemporary poetry has failed the educated reader: it is too selfish, too self-indulgent and obscure. By 'obscure' I do not mean 'difficult'. A difficult poem may reveal itself after a few close readings, or with the help of exegesis. Nor by 'obscure' do I mean 'mysterious' — we live in the midst of mystery. A poem can only be as simple as its subject matter. But the charge sticks. Many poets are making themselves irrelevant.

A poet 'captures' nothing — he is not a policeman! He presents us with moments won from the daily drudge; he brings us moments which surprise us, for revelation is always new. There is poetry in the air around us, in the games we play, in the daily intercourse of our lives. Poetry is never precious; it is vital and enabling. It is that which most puts us in touch with ourselves, with our environment. It is that which is unique within us. It is that which is indomitable and, therefore, ever free. Creative or destructive, it takes us beyond ourselves, our limitations; ever restless, it seeks out new adventure. As Emily Dickinson wrote:

> Exultation is the going
> Of an inland soul to sea,
> Past the houses — past the headlands —
> Into deep Eternity —

Bred as we, among the mountains,
Can the sailor understand
The divine intoxication
Of the first league out from land?

Poetry was, and is, a lonely occupation, an obsession born of inspiration. Too often have we heard the muse, the divine light, denied by pedants, poetry practitioners and poetasters. And their verse is the worse for it! Poetry is inspired and it is inspiring. There are only two criteria with regard to poetry — that it has something to say, and that it is well said. The rest we can consign to the critics!

Certainly, there are many good poems (and poets) in the anthologies of the literary Establishment. The purpose of this anthology, by complementing them, is to show the breadth and depth of contemporary Irish poetry. There is always an element of *uisce faoi thalamh*, a subterranean flow, about poetic endeavour that is often missed by the uninquisitive eye.

This, then, is an anthology of Irish poetry conceived, translated into English, or published in the 1980s, a decade that saw much poetic activity on this island — a decade that saw the death of Liam Miller and his Dolmen Press; a decade that saw the growth of poetry presses, Raven, Beaver Row, Dedalus, Salmon, Cló Iar-Chonnachta and Coiscéim, which have published many valuable poets for the first time. This is an anthology of Irish poetry *now*. Nowness by its very nature precedes (and takes precedence over) newness. Newness is a test of nothing. This is the poetry of today, with one eye cast (though not so coldly!) on Yeats and the Celtic revival, the other on the twenty-first century. There are others, however, whose muse is a purer Gaelic, and some indeed whose influences are 'European', American, or even Indian, Chinese or Japanese. Some too have turned their attention to the Islamic tradition, or set up echoes from Latin and Greek. These are the coordinates of Irish poetry *now*. I perceive my function as editor to present a selection of the best verse available from the best poets available, to show the range of this poetry, and to introduce the reader to some new voices.

It is an anthology of *Irish* poetry. By *Irish poets* I mean poets born in Ireland, poets of Irish ancestry, and non-nationals who have been resident in Ireland for long periods, who have an interest in Ireland and who have been published in Ireland. Leopold Bloom stated that 'A nation is the same people living in the same place ... or also living in different places.'

Patrick Galvin, living in a more consciously pluralist society, acknowledges the non-purity of nationality:

From these two I was born
The Ganges swaying with the Lee.

Nationality is a state of mind, an agreement. There is a citizenship of desire. The price of modern man's adaptability is his divided mind. This is the basis of his self-criticism which, destructively, leads to false assertions of national purity and, in extreme cases, to racism; creatively, it leads to art.

Much of this dividedness manifests itself in language — nowhere more so than in Ireland with its two languages, one tribal, ancestral, the other grafted to the old stock, both now part of the rose-bush that is Ireland. Moya Cannon speaks of the racial memory that calls on the reserves of the native tongue where 'the word comes when needed'. These 'small unassailable words/that diminish caesars' are part of the latent vocabulary of many non Irish-speaking Irish people to this day — these words are

a testimony
to waves succumbed to
and survived.

The native language can be generous, too, to the innocence and ignorance of the monoglot English speaker who must translate the native in terms of the imported. Thus Art Ó Maolfabhail, asked to give the English version of his name, will freely pardon '(an) ainnir adeir "What's that in English?"' Michael Coady's sympathy with the dead Job Wilks, an English soldier '... of the 56th Regiment, who died accidentally by drowning, at Carrick-on-Suir, 17th July 1868, in his 28th year' is further indicative of Ó Maolfabhail's injunction

Ní mór peacaí ró-ghránna
na staire a mhaitheamh
(But we must pardon/history's ugly sins).

13

Coupled with this willingness to forgive (and to be forgiven) — and John Liddy properly warns us of the dangers of easy absolution from 'confessors/Who would forgive us anything' — is the desire for justice. Indeed for many poets here included, the notion of justice goes hand-in-hand with religion and spirituality. In his poem for Father Romano, Desmond Egan alludes to

> ... the few
> who hand out like bread to others
> their ordinary life

whose own lives are testimony that 'the resurrection continues' despite the tyrannies that attempt to

> ... bundle truth into a jeep
> and stub out freedom with cigarette butts
> and build walls higher than the sky.

To both my own and Wolfhound Press' disappointment, Egan declined to be included in this anthology, consequent to a decision he made some time ago not to be represented in *any* anthology. (Another poet quoted above, Art Ó Maolfabhail, also declined, but his work is included in my *An Crann faoi Bhláth/ The Flowering Tree*, Wolfhound Press 1991.)

A welcome phenomenon of the nineteen-eighties was the coming to prominence of so many gifted women poets. To this day, despite their emergence (from small presses, notably the Salmon, Coiscéim and Beaver Row) they have received scant attention, critical or otherwise. Máire Bradshaw's *Box (of poems) Under the Bed* may be

> a monument
> to burnt potatoes
> and overcooked
> beef

but it is also her 'emancipation'. I feel that the Irish language, mindful of its traditions, has had a greater welcome for its women than English. A poet like Máire Mhac an tSaoi has been influential since the nineteen-fifties when her first collection, *Margadh na Saoire*, was published. At this time, her sister poets in English were, mainly, condemned to silence by the other great censorship of the time — the censorship of women and womanhood.

In its censorship of literature and women, Ireland was manifesting a narrowness, a single-mindedness inimical to the maturity appropriate to a *free state*. In the new state that the gombeens, as Michael D. Higgins reminds us, decided 'Was a good thing/Even for business', an alternative to the official view, the party line, was, at best, suspicious. The divided mind, that nagging in the conscience that was necessary for the liberation of women (and poets) was, seemingly, anathema to the patriarchs of the time. It has taken until now for Ireland to utter, in the words of Brian Friel's Hugh in *Translations*, that 'confusion is not an ignoble condition'. In achieving their freedom of utterance, their emancipation, poets like Moya Cannon, Joan McBreen, Rita Ann Higgins, Caitlín Maude, Áine Ní Ghlinn, Mary O'Donnell and others not only articulate an area of consciousness, of humanity hitherto unavailable from most poetry presses, they strike a blow for the liberation of consciousness in general.

Many of the poems are concerned with death — the death of family, of language, of traditions, of love. Dermot Bolger's *Lament for Arthur Cleary*, more than most, I feel, encapsulates the great loss of death. This is no regurgitation of the *eros-thanatos* motif — in itself, perhaps, an indication that Irish poetry has come out from the penumbra of Yeats. Using an eighteenth-century Irish lament (Eibhlín Dhubh Ní Chonaill's *Caoineadh Airt Uí Laoghaire*) as model, he translates modern Irish urban experience — drug abuse, money-lending, crime — with one eye on the older, rural, Gaelic tradition. Here is a true meeting of traditions, languages, cultures and literatures. If the poem ends with the death of Arthur Cleary, nonetheless the survivor, his lover

> will breathe (his) name
> On the lips of another's children
>
> Like a secretive tongue
> They will carry in their hearts
> To the foreign factories
> In which their lives will pass.

Translated into European terms, and how appropriate it is that Tomás Mac Síomóin, writing *as Gaeilge*, admits a European dimension here, the fate of Paul Celan serves as a reminder that death shall have no dominion, the grave no victory:

> ... féach, a Celan, fuil chraorag do chroí
> A' sileadh thar chab mo dháin
> Is an síol a chuiris fadó riamh
> Ag scoilteadh leac an bháis
>
> (... Celan, see your heart's red blood
> Spurt across this lip of Gaelic verse;
> See the seed you planted then
> Split the mould of death.)

Though life may be, in Dermot Bolger's words, a 'new enslavement' and the Irish in diaspora, Arthur Cleary, like Art Ó Laoghaire and Paul Celan, survives like 'the word (that) comes when needed ... its accuracy steadying the heart' (Moya Cannon, 'Taom').

I make no claim for this as a 'representative' anthology of contemporary Irish poetry. There are many anthologies widely available which make that claim. It is an anthology of poetry not generally available in the anthologies of the literary Establishment. The poetry in this anthology, drawn from the two languages on this island, is as diverse as it is delightful. Poetry, at its most powerful, is that which we believe in. Unlike the various deities who are (or were!) eternal, poetry is *made* by men and women and children, as indeed are religions. Work of human hands, we believe in poetry (or religions) when we sense the presence of the true, the good, the beautiful. These are poems I believe in. In presenting them, I urge the reader to open up to the offerings here. Here is poetry, luminous and lyrical. Enjoy!

Gabriel Fitzmaurice
Moyvane

DERMOT BOLGER

Born in Finglas in 1959, Dermot Bolger is a poet, novelist and playwright. He was co-founder and later director of Raven Arts Press, and is now executive editor of New Island Books. Among his publications are the novels *The Journey Home* and *Emily's Shoes*, and poetry collections *The Habit of Flesh* (Raven Arts Press), *No Waiting America* (Raven Arts Press 1982) and *Internal Exiles* (Dolmen Press 1986).

---

from *The Lament for Arthur Cleary*

My lament for you Arthur Cleary
As you lay down that crooked back lane
Under the stern wall of a factory
Where moss and crippled flowers cling

To stone crested by glass and wire
With a runlet of blood over your chest
When I raced screaming towards you
Hearing their cluster of boots retreat

I cupped your face in my palms
To taste life draining from your lips
And you died attempting to smile
As defiant and proud as you had lived

Behind me I could hear the cry
Of an engine kick-starting to life
And vanishing through laneways
Where we had rode on autumn nights

May it have led them mesmerised
Beneath railway bridges to the river

And skidded over oily cobbles
To drown those who killed its master

You were the only man I knew
The rest were all dancing clones
Lions swaggering in packs
Kittens petrified on their own

Unable to glance at a girl
Unless cocky with drink or stoned
But you stared into my face
Caught in the strobe lights alone

Not leering or smart-assed
Nor mumbling like a blushing bride
Leading me onto that floor
Where firm hands brushed my thighs

Confettied light combed our faces
From spinning globes of speckled mirrors
When we walked towards the exit
Through those swirling ranks of dancers

Beyond the cajoling disc jockey
And nervous girls trying to look bored
Away from the slow crucifixions
I had witnessed stranded on that floor

Our ears still hissing with static
We moved out into the tense nightscape
Past the crumpled stalks of drunks
Falling between the dispersed sheaves

Of crowds swept from discotheques
The glazed lovers with no place to stay

Queuing under the gaze of bouncers
In O'Connell Street's honky-tonk cafes

Sombre guardians and liberators
Stood paralysed in bird-stained bronze
While you unchained your Yamaha
And gave me the only helmet to put on

I accepted it like a pledge
And my arms circled your leather jacket
Your hair blown into my face
We raced up the quays towards my estate

Down a lane choked with scrap
Among the rust-eaten ghosts of lorries
Within sight of my father's house
Is where I first loved Arthur Cleary

With gems of slivered glass
Sparkling in light from a gypsy caravan
I unpeeled my black sweater
And felt a nipple harden on his tongue

Deserted streets had lightened
Before I undressed in exhilaration
And lay jaded beside my window
To catch the first blue notes of dawn

That blurred into whiteness
Where he lay curled against my back
His limbs climbing onto me
Until I woke by myself sopping wet

***

On your new motor bike
In the April days after we met
I would slip my hands
Into the warmth of your jacket

And watch blurred tar
Spinning backwards beneath us
As we rode past Ballymun
Through a green maze of tunnels

Crazily paved with light
Shaken from everlapping branches
Above the twisting roads
That swept downwards to Skerries

Ignoring the dichotomy
Between your words and what I saw
Because my pulse thrilled
In the slipstream of your world

But that world was dead
Though you could not realise it
A grey smudge of estates
Charted the encroaching horizon

Whose listless children
Staring you down when we passed
Were the future forming
Behind windscreens of stolen cars

Gone were the fistfights
And the flash of steel combs
The bolted flats sweated
Under the reign of shotguns

As you drew your legacy
In a Victorian labour exchange
And watched each friend
Succumb to emigration or jail

***

Grief is a knot
That is choking my throat
Rage is a whirlwind
Imploding through my skull

If only I had known
Your life to be in danger
I would have clawed
My way between you and them

I would have bitten
Into their skin with my teeth
I would have stubbed
Out their eyes with my nails

If only I had shouted
When you walked from the flat
Or ran to the balcony
Still naked to call you back

You went down steps
Because the lift was broken
You paused outside
And strolled out of my life

Across a courtyard
Where housewives were talking
Lying between sheets
I could hear the engine start

I drifted into sleep
To see a horse come riderless
Over fields trailing
A bridle smeared with blood

Towards a white house
Where a woman stood screaming
As I shuddered awake
I realised her voice was mine

I ran into the street
Where small clusters gathered
Whose eyes avoided me
When I raced frantically past

Guided by the silence
To the narrow tumbledown lane
In which singing blades
Had ended their intimate work

I knew they'd get you
Down some alleyway like that
Ringed by silent gangs
With both the exits blocked

You never knew fear
And that caused your death
Trusting the familiar
You roared into their trap

You'd become an exile
Caught in your native city
Whose police eyed you
Distrustful of neutrality

The dealers watched
Hating your open contempt
And kids growing up
Dreamt of your motor bike

Secretly dismantled
For new needles and deals
They hovered waiting
Every morning you left me

One Friday a lender
Arrived menacing at our flat
Hunting a neighbour
You grabbed his black folder

Releasing the pages
To scatter down into the yard
Like fugitive planets
From an exploding white star

That would eclipse us
Within its relentless orbit
I watched loose pages
Flutter into death warrants

That you just ignored
In sleep I saw charred corpses
I could not recognise
And clutched you till you woke

Begging you to leave
Now while we still might escape
You smiled back at me
Listening to late night traffic

And said in wonderment
My love I have finally come home
Then curled against me
As if love could save us from harm

***

My lament for you Arthur Cleary
And for the life which we led
For your laughter given freely
From those blood stained lips

In that year we lived as one
Without priest or registrar
To bless the ringlets of sweat
That tied our limbs together

I will not put on black
And spin out my life in mourning
I will breathe your name
On the lips of another's children

Like a secretive tongue
They will carry in their hearts
To the foreign factories
In which their lives will pass

When loud sirens scream
Across the European continent
And they walk into dawn
Towards scrubbed dormitories

They will tell the fable
Of the one who tried to return
And ride a glinting bike
In a final gesture of freedom

And think of early light
Slanted down that crooked lane
When their ancestor fell
And the new enslavement began

Berlin/Dublin: Nov/Dec, 1985

PAT BORAN

Pat Boran was born in Portlaoise in 1963. Winner of the Patrick Kavanagh Award in 1989, he has published *The Unwound Clock* (Dedalus 1990), *History and Promise* (IUP 1991), a collection of stories *Strange Bedfellows* (Salmon 1992) and *Familiar Things* (Dedalus 1993). He is editor of *Poetry Ireland Review* and is currently working on a novel.

---

return of *The Castlecomer Jukebox*

And even if we listen to ourselves so much
we hear nothing of the world about us;
and even if our pockets are always empty
and our calendars full of disappointments;
there will always be some youngster, wiser
by our foolishness, with a coin he has kept
for just the right time — when the dancing
has stopped and the jukebox light is gone out.

EVA BOURKE

Born in Germany, Eva Bourke has published two poetry collections to date, with a third collection, *Asylum*, in preparation. She is editor of *Writing in the West*, the literary supplement to the *Connaught Tribune* in Galway.

Litany for the Pig

Sorrowful and pale brother,
sister, sacrificed
countless times,

your name — sullied,
dragged through the mud
for thousands of years —
be praised.

Most generous of all creatures,
you give yourself totally.

Noble pig,
pig undefiled,
pig beloved by many nations,
immaculate pig!

Once you reigned in the chestnut forest,
the closed garden of purity
in a coat of dark fur,
energy bristling on slim flanks,
wrathful and protective
parent of striped princelings.

Savant and high-priest,
worshipped and devout,
trotting on split hooves
over the tiles of sinking temples
as swiftly
as through the padded grounds
of airy, leafy dominions,

the earth took you
into soft miry arms,
rocked you in warm ponds,
gave up to you only
its black buried wonder,
the rotting velvet of the truffle.

You were mother
of cunning and kindness
when you arrived,
an emissary from great distance,
light as Ariel,
your body the simple curved outline
and firmness
of a water jug,
your white-lashed eyes
full of wit and knowledge
of other worlds.

The word made flesh,
you dwelt among us,
but we closed our ears
to your message.

The deaf president didn't hear,
nor the philosopher of the taverns,

not the soldier,
nor the professor.

And now it's too late.
You were free,
so we crushed you.
We insulted you with our refuse,
you who was used to a diet
of acorn and sage,
chestnut and wild thyme.

You had to become more like us,
naked, exposed, fearful.

Torn limb from limb,
you're no more
than a grotesque swelling fruit,
squashed into stinking prisons
breeding generations of slaves.

Captive, trembling,
and devoured,
silent lamb to the slaughter —
your heart is broken.

MÁIRE BRADSHAW

The Box under the Bed (1986) was one of Máire Bradshaw's first poems and has been followed by her collections *Instinct* (1988) and *Hightime for all the Marys* (1992). Her poem *First Citizen / Free Woman* was commissioned for the conferring of the Freedom of Cork City on President Mary Robinson.

The Box under the Bed

I have taken my box
    from under the bed
      and placed it
        in the middle of
          the kitchen floor

a monument
    to burnt potatoes
      and overcooked
      beef

my emancipation
    my secret laid bare
    for all to
      see

go man
    wash your own
      socks

i am busy
    sorting out
      my ten year old
        rubbish of words.

RORY BRENNAN

Born in 1945, Rory Brennan grew up and was educated in Dublin, taking a degree in English and History from TCD. He has lived for long periods in Morocco and Greece and has worked in education, broadcasting and arts administration. He has had two books published, *The Sea on Fire* and *The Walking Wounded*.

---

from *Ten Sketches from a Greek Terrace*

The Abandoned Farms

From Lesbos to the Blaskets it's not hard to find
Roofless cottages explaining the scrapped hulks
Of trawler or caique listing on the sand,
A seized crane and a mine of tackle
Venomous with rust their field-gun monument.
History files this under the Marshall Plan
When plentiful labour in the cities meant
The chop for subsistence farmer, fisherman,
An old folks home in every dwindling village.
Yes, yes, nostalgia's cheap — try hauling a clogged net
Or hoeing iron earth. The old here were the last
To break their backs. The land's worth money now. Yet
Only a fool would wish them back their past,
Only another this dismantled age.

PADDY BUSHE

Born in Dublin in 1948 and educated at UCD, Paddy Bushe taught in Waterville, Co Kerry until 1991. Collections published to date are *Poems with Amergin* (Beaver Row Press 1989), *Teanga* (Coiscéim 1990) and *Counsellor* (Sceilg Press 1991). He has finished a new collection and is currently working on a collection of archaeological poetry.

---

from *Poets at Smerwick*

In November 1580 an expeditionary force of 600 Italian and Spanish soldiers landed at Smerwick, Co. Kerry, to aid the Irish rebel forces. They fortified the site of an older fort called Dún an Óir, or Fort Del Oro. The fort was besieged and captured by English troops under Lord Grey. On his orders, the expeditionary force was massacred, and their bodies thrown over the cliffs. Some Irish soldiers and camp followers were tortured and hanged. Elizabeth commended Grey for his decision, regretting only that he had spared some officers.

(i) — Positions

'Then put I certyn bandes who streight fell to execution.
There were 600 slayne'
(Lord Grey's report to Elizabeth)

This is the bare statement.
Details linger in other gleanings.
How the weapons were dented
from an excess of hacking.
How, at the forge, two men
bones hammered on an anvil,
died for three days. Such details
in flat prose can be swallowed
until the prose throws up two names
previously castled among the trees of the Blackwater,

silver poets of a golden age:
Ralegh snug in anthologies, Spenser ingenuously
singing the praises of his Faerie Queen.

    But at Smerwick, Edmund Spenser, secretary,
scripted beautifully Lord Grey's report;
Walter Ralegh, captain, organised the kill.

(ii) — Echoes

Smerwick. A hard Norse ring to it.
Fire and ice beat out the shape.
Raiders with reddened eyes and salted lips
named it, leaving echoes

among cliffs like sharp arbitrary edges.
These heights, those angular consonants
echo no woods, frame no soft vowels.
This is no Blackwater Valley. Here the bones lie out.

(iii) — Sonnet

The prisoners were penned inside the fort,
an open challenge to Elizabeth.
And Grey, as Spenser wrote in his report,
thought her best served by their exemplary death.

Thus Walter Ralegh, captain, part-time poet,
was ordered in to organise the work.
To gut six hundred men was heavy going,
but Ralegh thought it out like any clerk

compiling figures. Every man would kill
his share. In order that there'd be no doubt
he'd have to show the carcasses to fill
the quota Walter Ralegh had worked out.

The body count came out at five per man:
that tidy mind would make a sonnet scan.

(v) — Fool's Gold

Dún an Óir. Fort del Oro.
Named for gold that wasn't there.
Strange now Ralegh blundered
towards the scaffold, a lifetime later
sailing up the Orinoco for gold, no gold,
for El Dorado. Fort del Oro.
Dún an Óir. Beginning
towards an end. Blood and gold
like the slashed crimson trunks
of a courtier dancing in
and out of favour.

(vii) — Question

A question, Edmund Spenser:
what's the difference between an allegory
and a massacre? Between
a gentil knight pricking on the plaine
and the grating of a pike against a pelvis?
Between a marriage hymn on the Thames
and pregnant women hung at Smerwick?
Between your knight's iambic horror
at *a donghill of dead carkases he spide*
and your manuscripted parchment, sealed and signed?

CATHERINE BYRON

Born in London in 1947 to an Irish mother and English father, Catherine Byron was brought up in Belfast and educated at various convent schools and at Somerville College, Oxford. She has lived and worked in Scotland and England as writer and farmer. She has published three poetry collections, *Settlements* (1985), *Samhain* (1987) and *The Fat-Hen Field Hospital* (1993), and an autobiographical prose work, *Out of Step: Pursuing Seamus Heaney to Purgatory* (1992).

The Black and Tans Deliver her Cousin's Son

Galway 1921

'Didn't she step out into the yard
God love her
and see her own son's brains
scattered like mash about the flags?
And didn't she then kneel down
and gather the soggy shards
of her womb's child into her apron
carefully, as a girl gathers
mushrooms in the September fields?
And didn't she then stifle
the outbreath of her grieving
till only a whistle
or whimper of her lamentation
was heard in that place lest
the soldiers note her the more?'

Shears

In the linen mills I was a weaver of linen.
(That was before I married Billy Morrow.)
My own loom, uh huh, my own web.
Them was great times. Forty of us girls
pedalling Belfast linen on forty looms.

But yer man — Robinson, was it? — would saunter along
the aisle of the looms. Didn't he have the quick eye
for a slub in the damask, even a thickened thread.
He had soft hands. The other checkers 'd point
so as you could mend it. Robinson? Oh no.

His wee white nail 'd
pick and pick and pick
till that slub was a hole in the web
and the pink prick of his finger
poked right through.

'Yon's a fault!' Robinson dandered his shears
handy like, at his belt. In four snips
he'd cut the warp in two. 'That'll larn ye.'

Mebbe a day's piece gone. Mebbe a week's.
Whatever it was, it was a ruin of linen.
Priceless. The girl wageless. And in debt for the yarn.

KATHLEEN CAIN

Kathleen Cain is an Irish-American poet and writer whose work has appeared in several anthologies and periodicals. She has been a contributing editor for the *Bloomsbury Review* since 1982. She was born in Nebraska and graduated with a BA in English from the University of Nebraska-Lincoln. In 1984 a poetry fellowship from the Colorado Council on the Arts and Humanities allowed her to travel to Ireland. *Luna: Myth and Mystery,* an examination of the moon in human history, was published in 1991. She is currently working on a book about solstices and equinoxes. Among her collections are *Self-Conscious* (Celtic Rose Press), *1884, The First Year Out* (Mesilla Press) and *Late Bloomers* (Now It's Up to You Publications, Denver 1987).

Late Bloomers

It's the first time together like this
in years, coming home to these small places
where everybody but us
got a job as a waitress in high school.
Late Bloomers. The scientist, the lawyer,
the executive, and the poet.
We've come for coffee and blessings,
a show of faith if not love,
a willingness to test the pulse.
Coffee cups rise and fall
around us, that old sound as comfortable
as a gate closing on a summer yard.

Late Bloomers
never learn to crawl
never learn baby talk.
One day they just get up and dance, singing.
The whole time, singing.

It hurt
when the boys came around mouthing those new words
even our mothers didn't know how to look up.
All those brown summers, our first words to them
were as soft as the wind finding the elm trees.
We never could describe those words, but we knew
what the elm trees sounded like. We could give
the breezes a name. Some of us always whispered.
The rest of us had those loud voices that our mothers
warned us would drive people away. 'And
BIOLOGY? BIOLOGY? I'd hoped you'd take
Sewing. Or Home Ec. You'll *need* those.'

    Late Bloomers never learn to cook well
    before the age of thirty.

If we were late coming to our own lives,
we were always there first for others, all the eldest
daughter, eldest child. There were babies
behind us, every one, but where they tried
to make mothers of us too soon, they failed.
We became Late Bloomers instead.

    Late Bloomers always have mothers
    who think their daughters are just a little bit more mature
    than the rest.

We held on to what we could, each other
mostly. This gathering proves it.
Between us we've been through two wars,
five husbands, the shooting of a pope
and two presidents. Lovers remember us
by our eyes, or our teeth, or some mark on the body
only they have been able to find.

Late Bloomers never kiss and tell.
They just walk full-blown into
bad marriages, love affairs that fail,
or the arms of men who can't possibly love them.

We are always naming lovers, as if there were
some power in it. And if there isn't,
maybe we will bring it back.

Late Bloomers sort their lives out
as if something important
were just about to happen.

And when the postcard comes from you, it says
you're in Mexico, that you've started a new life,
and I'm reminded how I promised this poem
months ago. You will all understand.
You know how I am about promises.

Late Bloomers never make a promise
they can't keep, within twenty years.

Fern

There is no lesson in the fern
except uncurling slowly,
one green frond at a time;
learning to do well
in dark places;
letting growth come
from the underside of things.

SIOBHÁN CAMPBELL

Born in Dublin in 1962, Siobhán Campbell's poetry has been published in journals and anthologies including *Orbis, Cyphers, Quarry Special Issue of Irish and British Poetry, Hard Lines 3, Pillars of the House* and the *Irish Press*. She has read as part of the *Poetry Ireland* Introductions series, and at Sin É and Nuyorican Poet's Café, New York and has a first collection in preparation.

Miner

Once I used dread the dark, the hardness,
how it could catch me watching my own smallness
or listening for fear (my second heartbeat),
always listening for the quiet crack of an opening
or the low rumble of stone.

We believed that we lived on the brink of the terrible
toughened with the strength of overcoming fear
and every month brought gories from South Africa —
of parallel collapse, of poorly slatted shafts,
of glory for our brothers underground.

Then we would go threading women in the town,
travel for hours in the hot jittering dust
to find that women only want a drunkard
or a clown and soon I began to stay behind.

They hate to call me miner as I have no miner's wife
and mothers fear to leave me with their sons.
But I go below where I can tell the light
that fades a lady blondly from my eye and where I know
a pure one when she draws me through the deep.

Sometimes I have been down so long
I yearn to sink inside her and be gone.
I know some morning I may be found out.
They will come upon me where I lie
prostrate, naked, my fingers in her mouth.

The Chairmaker

I have been tempted to rush the job
to cut, not shave; to glue, not join
but when I stand beside it
and it's a friend or when I sit astride
and it's solid as a past, then I know
I am right to bide my time.

When people ask me how, I say
'My lady knows, she bakes loaves of bread.'
I tried that too until she said
if I kept opening the oven door
her rise would fall.

So I went back out to my shed
and dreamt myself a piece of elm.
I watched its wave and fingered its swell
and started to work slow as you like
letting my bevel follow the grain.

But this straight back kept coming up long
thinned as it came until almost a pole.
I kept going although it was strange,
honing the shaft and slatting the seat
which was high and tiny and more like a tray.

She came to me when the loaves were done
as if to make up for forcing me out.
She looked at it and her eyes were lit,
'A bird table! We can put it outside,
sit on your chairs and watch them sing.'
And eat your bread, I said, (I felt obliged)
and that night was as good as it's ever been.

MOYA CANNON

Moya Cannon was born in Donegal and studied history and politics at UCD and at Cambridge. She now lives in Galway, where she teaches in a special school for adolescent travellers. Her first collection *Oar* was published in 1990 by Salmon and won the 1991 Brendan Behan memorial prize.

Oar

Walk inland and inland
with your oar,
until someone asks you
what it is.

Then build your house.

For only then will you need to tell and know
that the sea is immense and unfathomable,
that the oar that pulls
against the wave
and with the wave
is everything.

'Taom'

The unexpected tide,
the great wave,
uncontained, breasts the rock,
overwhelms the heart, in spring or winter.

Surfacing from a fading language,
the word comes when needed.
A dark sound surges and ebbs,
its accuracy steadying the heart.

Certain kernels of sound
reverberate like seasoned timber,
unmuted truths of a people's winters
stirrings of a thousand different springs.

There are small unassailable words
that diminish caesars;
territories of the voice
that intimate across death and generation
how a secret was imparted —
that first articulation,
when a vowel was caught
between a strong and a tender consonant;
when someone, in anguish
made a new and mortal sound
that lived until now,
a testimony
to waves succumbed to
and survived.

'Taom' is an Irish word which means 'an overwhelming wave of emotion'.

Crow's Nest

On Saint Stephen's day,
Near the cliffs on Horn Head,
I came upon a house,
the roof beams long since rotted into grass

and outside, a little higher than the lintels,
a crow's nest in a dwarf tree.

A step up from the bog
into the crown of the ash,
the nest is a great tangled heart;
heather sinew, long blades of grass, wool and a
     feather,
wound and wrought
with all the energy and art
that's in a crow.

Did crows ever build so low before?
Were they deranged, the pair who nested here,
or the other pair who built the house behind the
     tree,
or is there no place too poor or wild
to support,
if not life,
then love, which is the hope of it,
for who knows whether the young birds lived?

Votive Lamp

The pope and the sacred heart
went off on the back of a cart,
and I've tried to find a home
for the child of Prague.

If that lamp weren't the exact
shape of a brandy glass there might be some
     chance
that I'd part with it.

Small chance, though.

If I'd been brought up in the clear light
of reason,
I might feel differently.

But I often come home in the dark

and, from the hall door,

in the red glow
I can discern
a child's violin
and, coming closer,
a plover;
the photograph of a dead friend;
three hazelnuts gathered from a well;
and three leather-skinned shamans
who flew all the way from Asia
on one card.

I designed none of this and don't know whether
sacred objects and images tend to cluster
around a constant light,
or whether
the small star's constancy,
through other lives and other nights
now confers some sanctity
on my life's bric-a-brac.

SEAMUS CASHMAN

Born in Conna, Co Cork, in 1943, Seamus Cashman studied at St Colman's College, Fermoy, St Patrick's College, Maynooth, and at UCC. He worked in East Africa and Ireland as a teacher before becoming a researcher and book editor. He founded Wolfhound Press in 1974, where he is now publisher. *Carnival*, his first collection, was published in 1988; a second volume is in preparation. He co-edited *Proverbs and Sayings of Ireland* and *The Wolfhound Book of Irish Poems for Young People*.

The Mystery

Who is the wind
if not I, asked Amerghin of the wind.
For answer he heard white rushes
on a dark night, whisper;
his long beard kissed blue eyes
and warmed oakgrained cheeks.
When the wind died, he said
Who is the silence
if not I.
In the stillness was no reply.

In the twentieth century
after Christ's death (before that
was Amerghin)
I sat upon a rock in Connemara
and listened.
There was laughter in the wind
and the waves' excitement
ebbed to innocence upon the sand.
And beyond the waves
    beyond the wind

a wanton stillness still remained.
My body fused with clay.
My mind forsook contained the echo
    Who is the wind
      if not I
        if not I
          if not I

My Hero

You could put your fist (he wrote)
into the exit wound on his chest
and made me wonder why my eyes had never seen
        that far
like tracking dragonflies that skittle up-river and
        are gone
or looking at a face and never seeing the mind.

I have other dreams.
The only exit wound I saw was as a boy who knew
        the way
to the long field to guide a new curate
and as the injured man was lifted from the binder
watched white bones falling from his back.
I have never understood why they were white
among the gore of cloth and straw but that
a dying neighbour stirred imagination,
I don't remember shock or fear — just immense
        curiosity
a sort of learning, being old.

No. There are no bullets in my life.
Huddled up in my foxhole at the front lines
eardrums burst

I light my cigarette and smoke and smile.
There is now time to ask my questions
                and to ruminate unhurriedly.
No exit.
Here the silence becomes me. The dragonfly,
the rose, the welcome sky,
untouched by past or future tenses,

So why the complications?
We were bred on myth and magic bread
and loves untouched, no dreams political,
No routes unmapped —
We lived indifferent to our futures;
heroes and heroines were boys and girls
etched on marble, plate and earthenware,
What great adventures, voyages and visions!

It seems that being made us great.
They were the immortals, not some wretched potters
cowering in a trench and shot to hold a line
to test philosophies and might.

And I seem to have always known that
that little boy who cried 'Wolf!' had had the wit
to be a little boy crying 'Wolf!'
Did he believe or no? Who knows . . .
for even he was never sure.

No. I have decided, since there is no other way,
to end the jester's search for who or what or why
                I am. Or we.
To be should do. In that alone, long known
                simplicity
I am my hero, and observe in me
                universes of infinity.

A Final Fling

With both thanks and apology to Lu Hsun whose words and ideas I have plagiarized shamelessly here to serve my own needs but who might have understood

My heart is extraordinarily lonely
void of love and hate, sadness, colour, sound or joy.
I must be growing old.
It is true my hair is going white. If so,
my soul's hair is surely whitening too?

But did I not grow old a hundred years ago?

Before that my heart was full of iron song,
passion's blood and fight and fall and resurrection
until one day it abandoned me.
I think it was some woman was the cause
for it happened after one had given up
on immobility. But even so, it came
and all that I have left is hope,
a shield against the dark night's love of fear
hanging on my body's walls.
Hope, and behind it, youth and memory.

O, I remember moonlight, stars and butterflies,
owls and flowers and laughter —
Not really how I see it now from this final hillock;
[Why now so lone. Have all the people
of the world grown old before me?
Old and safe for life's maternity.]
'Despair, like hope,' a good friend, dead, assured,
'is but another vanity.' Is it not sad that his memory
is still alive in me. He should be all forgotten
to round off his once-ness.

I would have a last great fling in my old age.
Even if I cannot find the youth outside.
Is it they sit calmly on the college greens,
thinking time away. Peaceful empty smiling.
If they cannot make me care, who ever will?
They cannot see this fight or they would surely rise
in angry love, destroy, create, re-live, re-die?
Arise!

I can hear those hollow mucus tubes
frightening the lives out of everyone
as they wait for me to go.
They do not know that this is my last fling,
this surging, deeply gasping, breathing
searching everywhere for air.

I hold those ugly sounds so full and live to me.
Inward — snortings, gurglings, scrapings;
outward — hisses
— as this great gasbag husky hollow diseased chest
deflates . . . I will not let it go —

Time now has gone. Just massive breathings,
and my mind. I do not believe —
I cannot summon god to hedge my bets.

So this is how I go —

My heart is full of an extraordinary loneliness
and there is no one there to know
that this is my last fling!
To cheer.

To go . . . I go . . . go —

GLENDA CIMINO

Born in the United States, Glenda Cimino moved to Ireland in 1972, almost by chance, a poet drawn by the music of Irish placenames: Mullinacuffe, Tinahely, Shillelagh. In 1980 she co-founded Beaver Row Press in Dublin. In 1988, her first book of poetry, *Cicada*, was published in Dublin. She is currently working on a local Florida newspaper while she pursues research for a writing project, but she is still based in Dublin.

What the Court Clerk Said

When I was a girl
the land was free
we had our houses
far apart
and rode horses.
there was no dam
and the river
flowed freely.
I never saw
a policeman
and a white man
seldom
which was often enough.
we spoke
our own beautiful
words.
today
our houses
are back to back
with cement in between
there are not so many
horses

the river is gone
there are many police
many white men
and many drunken Indians.
my children
go to school
they learn English
and forget
their own tongue.
I must work here
and my husband
is a policeman.

(Rosebud Reservation, South Dakota, 1970)

Sioux Vision

The Indians
have been made
Curios
in their own land
their holy places
are crowded
with sightseeing buses
yet on the Sioux reservation
under a cloudless sky
young Willard Eagle Thunder
looks toward the Black Hills
and cries, 'Look! Can't you
just see
Sitting Bull and Crazy Horse
galloping toward us?'

(Rosebud, 1970)

The Unwed Wife
(for Brian)

Four a.m. The coldest hour. Our child sleeps beside me,
her soft petal breath warming the sheets
where you have been. She entitles me to nothing;
her whole being radiates love.

After six months' absence, the pillow again
smells sweetly of you. But for five nights
I have gone to sleep and woken without you.
When will I stop counting the lonely nights?

I sleep in my clothes and dream of nakedness
with you. My dream of you is your best part.
The day I stop dreaming you, you will surely disappear.
You don't know how my dreams keep you going.

My powerful woman's magic draws you near
when the moon is full, as moon draws sea,
as its power causes solid land to ebb and flow,
imperceptibly .... In the space between wish and lie

Is my poem's truth. Our daughter's hand holds the blanket,
the tilt of her chin so like yours.
Beside the bed, the book you were reading and a peach,
perfect in light and shadow as a Rembrandt.

Tonight I have locked the doors; I am too far away
to hear your knock, real or imagined.
Sirius in his own lonely exile guards our door.
I think of reading the book. Eating the peach.

Outside the trees stretch in the wind.
Without you we sleep always in the light.
Darkness may not penetrate our white sanctuary.
When you come you bring darkness, want the light off,

You wear your pain like a skin you cannot remove,
you are always on the prongs of a dilemma.
You never love me enough to stay;
I don't know why you come.

But tonight, where your head rested,
your smell sweetly scents the pillow.
Soon, in the gray morning, I must arise
and wash it away.

MICHAEL COADY

Michael Coady was born in Carrick-on-Suir in 1939 and has lived there since. The author of two collections from Gallery Press, he gained the Patrick Kavanagh Award in 1979, and Arts Council Bursaries in 1981 and 1988. He is currently engaged in exploring areas of creative connection between poetry and prose, memory and time, people and place.

Though There Are Torturers

Though there are torturers in the world
There are also musicians.

Though, at this moment, men
Are screaming in prisons
There are jazzmen raising storms
Of sensuous celebration
And orchestras releasing
Glories of the spirit.

Though the image of God
Is everywhere defiled
A man in West Clare
Is playing the concertina,
The Sistine Choir is levitating
Under the dome of St. Peter's
And a drunk man on the road
Is singing for no reason.

The Jackdaws of Chapel Street

the jackdaws of chapel street
don't care much either way
for weddings, births or funerals
or what the people say

they perch on roofs and chimney-stacks
and watch processions pass
the drunken and the dead man
the crowd from sunday mass

they cast a grey and empty eye
upon the play below
they nest and feed and squabble
while generations go

the grieving man behind the hearse
looks up to see them pairing
above the cold stone statues
that wind and rain are wearing

the jackdaws of chapel street
don't care much for the people
but blithely shit on tombstones
and fornicate on steeples

Solo

The last movement
must be avant garde,
unscored and unaccompanied
by lover, friend or mother.

Since finally
you'll have to make it
      solo
and by ear

Now's the time —
with the dance still on
and the band swinging —

To stand up
and blow
ad lib
with all the wrong notes
you dare.

Letting Go

I love the abandon
of abandoned things

the harmonium surrendering
in a churchyard in Aherlow,
the hearse resigned to nettles
behind a pub in Carna,
the tin dancehall possessed
by convolvulus in Kerry,
the living room that hosts
a tree in south Kilkenny.

I sense a rapture
in deserted things

washed-out circus posters
derelict on gables,
lush forgotten sidings
of country railway stations,
bat droppings profligate
on pew and font and lectern,
the wedding dress a dog
has nosed from a dustbin.

I love the openness
of things no longer viable,
I sense their shameless
slow unbuttoning:
the implicit nakedness
there for the taking,
the surrender to the dance
of breaking and creating.

The Poppy in the Brain

— *They shall be remembered forever.*

1.
Chance preserved in someone's bric-à-brac
this fading studio dream
of a Home Counties beauty smiling
in soft focus with the legend
'Buy War Bonds and Feed the Guns'

under which indelibly
he'd pencilled all his innocence
before he met the shrapnel
and the wire

I hope you get this safe
im all rite and been treted well
you need not worry I have
good blankits and am warm.

2.
I don't know how next time
they'll feed you for it,
how they'll lace and flavour up
the same old bullshit —
but they'll find a way

they'll find a way

and though I'd like to feel
you kids are smarter now
and not for gulling, let me
not feed you bullshit of my own,
while knowing in my heart's dismay
you'll line up and obey,

oh yes you will you know,
you always do —

you'll line up and obey.

Assembling the Parts

Standing in sunshine
by Highway 84
I'm photographing a factory
which is no longer there

looking for my father
by an assembly line
which has halted
and vanished into air

catching the sepia ghost
of a young tubercular Irishman
who's left a rooming house
at 6 a.m. in a winter time
during the Depression

when my mother is still a girl
playing precocious violin,
a Miraculous Medal under
her blouse, in Protestant
oratorios in Waterford.

A pallid face in the crowd
in a dark winter time,
he's coughing in the cold,
assembling typewriters
in Hartford, Connecticut,

waiting for blood on his pillow
to send him home, where he'll
meet her one ordinary
night with the band playing
Solitude in the Foresters' Hall.

Fifty years on
he's nine Septembers dead
and a tourist in sunshine
by Highway 84
is photographing a factory
which is no longer there,

assembling the parts
of the mundane mystery,
the common enigma of journeys
and unscheduled destinations,

the lost intersections
of person and place and time
uniquely fathering everyman
out of the random dark.

Job Wilks and the River

' ... *of the 56th Regiment, who died accidentally by drowning, at Carrick-on-Suir, 17th July 1868, in his 28th year.*'

I feel that I know you, Job Wilks —

no imperial trooper swaggering
these servile Tipperary streets
before my grandfather drew breath,
but a country lad out of Hardy,
drunk on payday and pining for Wessex,
flirting with Carrick girls
in fetid laneways after dark,

out of step on parade to Sunday Service
with comrades who loved you enough
to raise out of soldiers' pay this stone
which would halt my feet among nettles
now that jackdaws are free in the chancel,
Communion plate lies deep
in the dark of a bank vault,
and spinster daughter of the last

rector, in a home for the aged,
whispers all night to an only brother
dead these forty years in Burma.

How commonplace, Job Wilks, how strange
that this should be where
it would end for you, twenty-eight
summers after the midwife washed you.
With that first immersion
you took your part
in the music of what happens,
and an Irish river was flowing
to meet you, make you
intimate clay of my town.

On a July day of imperial sun
did your deluged eyes find
vision of Wessex, as Suir water
sang in your brain?

I know the same river you knew, Job,
the same sky and hill and stone bridge:
I hope there were Carrick girls with tears
for a country lad out of Hardy,
drunk on payday and pining
for Wessex.

The Land and the Song

> *'Cad a dhéanfaimid feasta gan adhmad?*
> *Tá deireadh na gcoillte ar lár.'*

When Jack of the Castle, the last of Kilcash, was buried
A merchant from Carrick bought furniture, flooring and
    roof,
The great who had lived in the place were ghosts in a poem
Sung under thatch in a tongue that was beggared and
    doomed.

Only the beaten sang, to remake their story,
To shape a lost self, draw sweetness out of decay;
The strong were never the singers of vanished glory,
Their land was their truth, their poem the power that it
    gave.

Always this matter of land, its having and holding
Whatever the banners that waved under Slievenamon,
Power lay in fields, however the quarrel was clothed,
This is the daytime truth of what's here and what's gone.

The state has planted a forest of pine and sitka
To yield an acceptable profit in fifty years,
Under the mountain the land and its story's rewritten
By men who own milking parlours and video gear.

The County Council may save the last walls of the castle
For tourists and sentiment tied to some phrase in the song,
Children who chant it at school are serving a piety —
Stammering sounds of lament in a broken tongue.

But out of the fallen woods and the unroofed silence
A dominion endures above unrelenting day —
This place was sung for its trees and a woman's kindness
And the song in itself is whole, and redeems its clay.

PATRICK COTTER

Born in Cork in 1963, Patrick Cotter has had two collections of poetry published, *A Socialist's Dozen* (Three Spires Press 1990) and *The Misogynist's Blue Nightmare* (Raven Arts Press 1990). Runner-up for the Patrick Kavanagh Award in 1988, he is editor of *The Steeple* poetry magazine and the *Cloverdale Anthology of Irish Poetry*.

The Unreformed Feminist Speaks Out

A diaspora of brown bread crumbs which have fled from a
                                          nibbling;
A bowlful of demerara sugar still patiently awaiting
Entry into the vapoury chamber of a teacup;
Chunky, *alternativ*, stoneware pottery holding solid ground;
Such are my soul companions
As I sit by my table at the Co-Op cafe,
Their invited guest.
Not that I am alone in this room by the river:
At a not too distant table, on the other side of the aisle
Behind the vase full of minority flowers
Sits the lesbian of my dreams.
The classical qualities of the bones of her face
Are refined by the young soldier's crewcut
She has recently acquired.
The lines of her body are tightly hugged by her stonewashed
                                          dungarees,
As tightly as I could hug if I might,
But I know I may not, may never,
And so all I can do is deliver the most incredulous stare,
Easily detectable evidence of my sinful infatuation.
I try to do it as she won't be too offended,
By making out I'm staring at the poster behind her head.

The poster is promulgating the believer's doctrine,
Reminding me how easily we men can be brutish without trying
Reminding me how we men can be as offensive as warty toads,
Merely by considering a woman to be the most beautiful creation
                                                    in the cosmos.
So I notice the beautiful creation is returning my stares,
Giving me glances too full of puzzlement to accommodate
                                                    disdain.
She knows my history of dining here.
She knows my professions of feminist *Politik*.
She's heard of the wounds I've collected,
The scorn of the crowd, the hatred of the slanderers
Because I've dared to preach dignity for men who love men.
All of this leads to an override of her commonsense
And all she can think is:
'Why is that fuckhead of a queen staring at me?'

TONY CURTIS

Tony Curtis was born in Dublin in 1955. He studied literature at the University of Essex and Trinity College Dublin. His first collection was *The Shifting of Stones* (1986), followed by *Behind the Green Curtain* (1988), both from Beaver Row Press. Forthcoming is *This Far North*. One of his poems is in *The Great Book of Ireland*.

The Suitcase

This is the Kilburn High Road
running up towards Cricklewood
away from England's Edgeware Road
where the homeless Irish come
carrying their father's battered suitcase,
although their father may have never left home.
They used to buy them at the summer fairs
for that day when their time would come,
or get them off a friend who died,
his lifelong journey finally done.
That's how my father stayed in his fields.
His suitcase travelled to him
from an Irish woman with a soft Kerry voice,
whose children's eyes were Irish blue
and accents East End Cockney.
She had married three times in England
and returned sadly widowed again.
The locals said 'she deserved what she got
the saintless, unGodly woman.'
Yet they listened discreetly to the stories she told,
of how one husband left in a blitz of booze,
another in a blitz of bombs,
the last one dying on a beach outside Calais

his toes never touching French soil.
She used to giggle at the thought,
said it reminded her of once
when he danced on Brighton beach
in nothing but his cotton drawers.
When she died the priest brought round her suitcase.
My father left it by the door.
In our kitchen someone was always leaving home.

PÁDRAIG J. DALY

Born in Dungarvan, Co Waterford, in 1943, Pádraig J. Daly is a member of the Order of St Augustine and is currently parish priest of Ballyboden, Dublin. His most recent book, *Out of Silence*, was published by Dedalus Press in 1993.

Sagart I

In many ways you're like an old man. Perhaps
You walk alone more than most people twice your age.
You notice each change of weather, the drift
Of smoke to sky. There is a certain decorum
You follow in your dress, the way you comb your hair.

You have many acquaintances, few friends;
Besides your unreplying God you have no confidant.
Nevertheless you lift your hat to all. Old ladies
Especially will seek you out, sometimes a sinner.
You are guest at many celebrations, a must at birth or
    death.

Sometimes you wonder whether this is how God intended
    it.

Sagart II

Every so often you withdraw,
Take twine, a dozen pegs,
And begin to mark off
A small exclusive corner
Of yourself.

But other people's cows
Come shoving against
Your walls and their chickens
Fall on your sprouting hedgerows;

And though you dig
Deep trenches all about
And festoon the place
With dangerflags,

People dumbly somehow
Stumble against it
And send you spinning
Farther and farther in along yourself
For peace.

Sagart III

Like old countrywomen
By fireplaces on Winter evenings,
We sit alone.

Outside day draws in; dogs
Bark to one another across acres
Of mountain; the last red hen
Goes wearily to shelter; younger
Voices rise and fall in laughter
Or argument; there is banging of churns
And milk poured quietly.

We have some urgent tale to tell
About life; but our mouths open
And no sound gathers shape.
We belong out by the side of things.

'Sagart' is the Irish for priest.

JOHN F. DEANE

Born on Achill in 1943, John F. Deane has had several collections published, the most recent in 1981, *The Stylized City*. Founder of *Poetry Ireland* in 1979, he now writes full-time and is editor of Dedalus Press.

Questions

He walks the roads of Achill, always with the same
old cap; we meet, he raises that cap to shout
confident assertions about earth or sky, then laughs

out of his belly. He has no tests to put
to life or God, but waits outside till sermon's done
to eye parades of jeans or blouse into his

church, then kneels on cap inside the door, great
red hand urging his chin to prayers. Between
wet dawn, dung-yard at dusk, death harries him

but he survives, whistling, though his eyes can sharpen
as peregrine's after prey, for he too, lives where cliffs
ride out naked, and mists visibly corrode; I

have questions I would like to ask him, but not now, not
    now.

Miracle in Thomas Place

Midnight light was freezing the back garden of number 9;
a man came out to piss before going to bed;
clouds tinted orange from the city lamps
passed, like lazy smoke-puffs, between man and moon;
the man pissed over a rose-bush,
put his hands in his pockets and hitched up his trousers;
stars were hanging about, some here some there;
he cleared his throat and spat into the rose-bush;
in the house beyond a bathroom light flicked off;
o the old, old earth, scaffolded on millions of years;
the pissing and spitting will pay dividends, come spring
    D.V.;
you can't be too careful these days, he said,
locking the door before going up to bed.

Missionary

Heavyweight wrestler for God, white beard
a waterfall down his soutane, he rose
like an old belfry above our novice years.

Stories he told us, colouring the edges
of our desert: witch-craft cowed by a lit
match, tribes by false teeth brandished; he

had crossed God's jungle carrying God's flag.
I wore a tightened cincture round my waist,
I lauded God round Kimmage grounds and heard

a voice from a blazing acacia bush call 'Whom
shall I send?' Where a white-flecked blackbird sang
I knelt and cried 'Lord here am I, send me, send me'.

Matins

We walked round shrubbery, cowled in silence,
somewhere in the long pause of mid-morning;
the fuchsia hung in scarlet, bees drew out
their honey; high trees benignly watched, long
used to circling figures on the gravel; we
read Rodriguez, his tome of huge wonders, deeds
of saints, glories of holiness, miracles
sprouting out of deserts. Secretly, I longed
that those naked whores spirited out of hell
into the monks' cells should tempt me, too;
I fasted, prayed, scaled the cliffs of sanctity
to no avail; always the sudden wren
distracted, a weed's unexpected beauty on a stone,
coolness of peas bursting against my palette; I
stayed in my tiny group, going round and round.

At a Grandmother's Grave

That I should perform this office for you, seemed
profanity, you who had watched me from a child
assume the black and white of a minister
of the eternal mysteries; you had performed
such servile duties for me, now you lay
coffined at my feet.

So I assumed a presence;
a childhood's incoherent love I distanced
from me, spoke in a grave, high tone: *De*
profundis clamavi ad te Domine.

Over my words hung a huge mid-morning
silence; beyond us the sluggish estuary, those
black-headed gulls about their squabbling; you
in that brown hole, I sprinkling water on you
from a plastic bottle.

In my monastery cell
that night I watched pale light outline
my cassock hanging on the door, its folds
deep-shadowed, its shapelessness a figure lost
among great wilderness.

Your face
is clay now; suburbs bulk around the cemetery
till view of the sea is lost; I stand, grateful,
with wife and child curb weeds from your small plot.

Sacrament

You, pictured for ever, before me;
I stand in black and wear a white
carnation; you, holding an array
of golden roses, maidenhair, smile up
at me and you are beautiful; your body
washed for me and gently scented;
you, set apart in white, a mystery,
all sacred;

> we are holding hands for ever,
dedicated; such the signs of a deep
abiding grace.

> Another image
graven on my mind; you lie, again
in white; on your breast a silken
picture of the Virgin; they have washed
your body, closed your eyes, you hold
no flowers; vein-blue traces
of suffering on your skin, your fingers
locked together, away from me.

But it is I who have loved you, known
the deepest secrets of your grace; I take
the golden ring from your finger; I kiss
the bride,

> and they close the heavy doors
against me, of that silent, vast cathedral.

The Blue Toyota Van

They set out to cross the world
in a blue Toyota van. At Chartres
Cathedral, exemplary stone saints
drift towards heaven, rose windows
filter difficult light; her thoughts,
like those of Heloïse, were not on prayer
but wantonness; the soul, between
deaths, needs love. In the carpark

at Altamira, above caverns with their
excavated silences, he knelt
before her; all through the night, under
a summer moon, bison and deer
were on the move, and men
stalked them, gathering the ochre
pigments of their art. They followed

the pilgrims' path to Compostella, the blue
Toyota van disturbing mountain
villages, road that coiled
between earth and heaven, where the living
toil shoulder to shoulder with the dead and sit
watching the turn of the world through endless
dusk. The bronze censer of Santiago

swung like a pendulum across the nave, banishing
sterility, hanging, the way the world
hangs in dark blue spaces. Above their heads
a ladder, precariously tilted, led
towards heaven; and small
petulant souls climbed up, their cries
the sharp cries of insects in the air while devils
keen as scorpions, stabbed at them endlessly.

They set out to cross the world
in a blue Toyota van; they made
love under its roof, parked by night
at the edge of sunflower fields, by day
where swallows trawled through a bright sky.

GREG DELANTY

Born in Cork in 1958, Greg Delanty won the Patrick Kavanagh Award in 1983 and the Allan Dowling Poetry Fellowship in 1986. He has been included in many anthologies including the *Field Day Anthology of Irish Literature 500 - Present* (Faber and Faber 1991) and *An Crann Faoi Bhláth/The Flowering Tree* (Wolfhound Press 1991). He has published two collections of poetry, *Cast in the Fire* (Dolmen Press 1986) and *Southward* (Dedalus Press/Louisiana State University Press 1992). He is currently working on two new titles: one is an anthology of contemporary poetry, which he is editing with Nuala Ní Dhomhnaill, and the other is his own next volume of poetry, *American Wake*.

Tracks of the Ancestors

(To Louis de Paor)

Along a boreen of bumblebees,
        blackahs & fuchsia
somewhere around Dunquin
        you said that Pangaea

split there first & America
        drifted off from Kerry
& anyone standing on the crack
        got torn in two slowly.

We never dreamed we'd end up
        on other continents,
hankering for familiar mountains,
        rivers or grey firmament.

Out where you've settled,
        the Aborigines
on walkabout recite dreamtime songs
        that signpost journeys.

Each shifting verse
    directs which way to go,
celebrating the rainbow serpent
    & whichever sky hero.

As we traverse our landscapes,
    whether bog, bush, prairie
or city, we are the walkabout,
    outcast Aborigine.

We can't identify where
    exactly we are from day to day,
but if we don't keep up singing
    we'll lose our way.

Out of the Ordinary

Skin-head pigeons strut in a gang
along the road's white line
& fly from under a fuming cop car.
Lazy, contented seagulls catch rides
on the conveyor belt of a river —
Others glide & hover in the slow air
of a busking tin whistle player
as if conjured from his upside-down hat.
Singing thrushes play on the fret board
of electric wires & sparrows
arrow upward, seemingly desperate
to enter heaven, not noticing heaven
has descended to the ordinary
as we saunter along Union Quay.

Tie

Without asking, you borrowed your father's black tie,
sure that he had another black tie to wear
should some acquaintance or relation die.
But had he? He should be here somewhere.
But where? Could he be at home on this dark day,
ransacking drawer after drawer for a funeral tie?
Yes, that must be what has kept him away.
Though you are sure you saw him, tieless,
smiling over at you, before you lost him again
among the keening cortege. Leaving you clueless
to his whereabouts, till earth, splattering a coffin
(or was it the wind ululating in each prayer?),
informed you that you can never give your father
back his black tie, though you'll find him everywhere.

While Reading *Poets in their Youth*

Reading by candle in the caravan
I'm disturbed by a moth fluttering
around my book & then the flame.
It drops with a waxen, burning smell
that reminds me of Icarus & Daedalus;
how I used to get the two confused
& how I've always wanted to know why
exactly moths are drawn to light;
why starlings batter themselves
at lighthouses & what safeguards
there are for those who fly by night.

THEO DORGAN

Born in Cork in 1953, Theo Dorgan has published *Slow Air* (Cork 1975), *A Moscow Quartet* (Dublin 1989) and *The Ordinary House of Love* (Galway 1991, reprint 1992). Editor of *The Great Book of Ireland* (1991) with Gene Lambert, and *Revising the Rising* (1991) with Máirín Ní Dhonnchadha, he is currently director of *Poetry Ireland/Éigse Éireann*.

All Souls' Eve

> *Deirid lucht léinn gur chloíte an galar an grá ...*
> *Nuair a théas sé fá'n chroí cha scaoiltear as é go brách.*

Once a year in a troubled sleep
That room stands drenched in light
Where I sit and watch us both asleep
In a cold sweat of fright.

A high room where the boards creak
The skylight faced with frost
Our bodies interlaced in sleep
And the world long lost.
Beside the bed my blue jeans
Lie crumpled in your dress
Dawn light coming in as we
Unconsciously caress.

The germ of death is in that dream
There in our mingled breath
There in our silence and our speech
— as when you moan *not yet*.
We lie in the breath of lovers lost
To the world since time began

Their souls the patterns in the frost
As you turn beneath my hand.

Once a year in a troubled sleep
I watch until we wake
... this is a vigil that I keep
And never must forsake
Until slow bells break
From a world long lost
Sleep-drugged lovers
To a city gripped in frost.

There is no time and all time
As we surface to a kiss
What we were before we died
A game compared to this.
No world and a whole world
In an innocent caress
Never again the same world
We leave when we undress.

> *The learned men say that love*
> *Is a killing disease.*
> *When it goes to the heart*
> *It will never come out again.*

SEÁN DUNNE

Seán Dunne was born in Waterford in 1956 and now lives in Cork where he works with the *Cork Examiner*. His books include poetry collections, *Against the Storm* (Dolmen Press, 1985) and *The Sheltered Nest* (Gallery Press 1992); an autobiography, *In My Father's House* (Anna Livia 1991); and he was editor of *The Cork Anthology* (1993). He has written essays and reviews for many publications in Ireland, England and the USA.

Morning at Mount Melleray

Woken for Lauds, I lie
Listening to water in the guesthouse garden.
Birdsong chips at the silence.
A gun barks to scare crows from fields.
The morning bell of Melleray booms
Over hills where fog thickens.

In the next county, you sleep in a house
High over cliffs and a packed harbour.
Perhaps our son is crying, his frail
Fists boxing the air until you arrive,
Breast-offering, warm, your cheek
Flushed where it pressed the pillow.

A monk reads in the long refectory.
Jugs of milk on wooden tables,
Plates of bread and cut cheese —
You would like such ordinary scenes
Where the clatter of plates is praise,
Each movement charged with meaning.

More spectator, voyeur, I kneel in doubt
Before the altar. A tabernacle shaped
Like a honeycomb gleams under sodium light.
The air is cold as Christ on a crucifix,
His silver legs bent and thin to my touch.
Brown as nuts, beads dangle from fingers.

In farmyards monks scrape dung from drains.
Cylinders turn in the laundry and sheets
Are pressed between rollers. Monks slide
Wood towards a chain-saw, shavings
Spit and snarl around hands.
Poring over books, a novice jots notes.

Here I am learning the meaning of love:
Your absence a contact some never know.
Gentle as drizzle, you move in my memory,
Your brush daubing a canvas for the true
Image you intuit at the heart of paint.
I sense that image in the silence now.

A monk at morning on a long walk talks
Of Eliot's rose-garden and chances missed.
I sense that door ajar, and you
Waiting among the roses, fingers pressed
Against petals of the *rosa mundi*.
Briars tangle the chances we failed to take.

In a long shed heavy with potato smells,
I touch and measure the miraculous bin.
Crowds called during famine and were fed
Meal until it flowed from tin
Basins broken with rust, or poured
From aprons laden like hammocks of grain.

The bin never emptied, but its flow
Filled those who walked for days
Over mountainsides stifled by famine.
I hear them talking in Irish, all
Keen to tell of the miracle at Melleray,
And I know how they felt at such abundance.

I ask for success in simple things:
Husband-ship and father-care, the deep
Patience of the monk with ancient texts
That blur and clear with meaning at last.
Everything has the sense of something planned,
Nothing is random or out of hand,

Insect and animal assume their places.
A speck climbs its Everest stalk.
The air at evening is meshed with midges.
The abbey cat drops an offering at my feet,
A dead bird, then guiltily walks away.
Fish dart and glitter in a fountain pool.

On a pathway in sunlight I think
Of the need for gentleness in our affairs.
Water sprays from spinning nozzles as I walk,
Drenching the parched vegetables.
I share that need with resurgent roots.
The refreshed stalks strengthen and grow.

Dear heart, our lives unroll like scrolls.
Lectio ends with the shutting of books.
Softly, women confess as shutters slide.
Old pain subsides and wounds are healed.
Stealing from the bakery, odours of bread.
I want to take your hands in mine and press.

Refugees, 1969

They swarmed South in trains and stayed
For weeks in a disinfected barracks.
The word *refugee* failed to fit those
Who walked around Waterford in salvaged clothes,
Or idled on benches chewing at matchsticks.
One scaled the side of a handball alley,
Threatening to leap into our local abyss.

Others fought in chip-shops or went on the piss
In pubs where nothing moved faster than clock-hands.
They were far from faces in a flickering crowd
Streaming from ghettoes as sirens wailed,
Or women stumbling from a bombed hotel
Waving bundles to a welcome of flashbulbs.
These were like ourselves. When they left
We waved like exiles from a boat drawing out.

The Bluebell Ring

Settled in a ring of bluebells, we watch
Pheasants search tail grasses for seed.
Hounds bay in kennels near the house
As if in protest at the last hunt's end.
Woods echo their cry that's tossed
Amplified back to deserted yards,
The shut stables where bales are stacked.
Nothing disturbs us but a bird

Clattering through trees until
Its song dominates the air — a keen
Whistling, sharp as a poacher's low
Signal sent in warning across weirs.
We could be Lord and Lady here, or mere
Butler and maid. In centuries-old light
We meet near the sun-dial and I press
Your face to mine as horses trot past.

We could plot escape, a boat to France,
Servants lugging our trunks to a cove.
On avenues horses whinny and we sense
Spies in the rustle of leaves and grass.
Instead we are merely ourselves, you
In a yellow dress with your hair spread
Loosely over bluebells as we talk.
I, eager to confide as you press my hand.

Settled in a ring of bluebells, we watch
The gardens empty as late light fades,
The spray of fountains stilled, hounds
Calmed by darkness covering yards.
The last bus grumbles through the gates
And we delve into woods towards the dark.
Courtly, precise, we arrange the ground.
Your dress slips from you without a sound.

GABRIEL FITZMAURICE

Gabriel Fitzmaurice was born in 1952 in Moyvane, Co Kerry where he now lives and teaches in the local National School. He has published eleven books to date including poetry in English and Irish, children's verse, an anthology of poetry in Irish with verse translations, *An Crann Faoi Bhláth/The Flowering Tree* (Wolfhound Press 1991) and collections of ballads and folksongs. His latest book of poetry is *The Father's Part* (Story Line Press, Oregon 1992).

Portaireacht Bhéil

Who would make music hears in himself
The tune that he must play.
He lilts the inarticulate.
He wills cacophony obey.

Garden

(For Brenda)

We were a garden dug by eager hands.
Weeds were swept by shovels underground.
Brown earth, blackened and split by Winter,
Was picked to a skeleton by starving birds.

Spring surprised us with a yelp of daisies
Defiant as a terrier guarding his home ground.
We planted seed in the cleft of drills
Slimy with earthworms.

Today I picked the first fruit of our garden.
Bloody with earth I offered it to you.

You washed it and anointed it,
We ate it like viaticum.

In the eating of pith and seed
I loved you.

In the Midst of Possibility

Now I love you
Free of me:
In this loving I can see
The YOU of you
Apart from me —
The YOU of you that's ever free.

This is the YOU I love.
This is the YOU I'll never have:
This is the YOU beyond possession —

The YOU that's ever true
While ever changing,
Ever new.

Now,
Naked
Free,
The YOU of you
Meets the ME of me
And to see is to love;
To love, to see:

In the midst of possibility
We agree.

Derelicts

Whenever I picture the village fools
They drool with the hump
Of benevolence on their backs.
Living in hovels as I remember
They had the health of the rat.

They perched on the street corner
Like crows around the carcass
Of a lamb. Stale bread and sausages
Would feed a hungry man.
Beady with the cunning of survival
Each pecked the other from his carrion.

Children feared them like rats in a sewer:
They stoned their cabins
And the stones lay at the door.

Like priests they were the expected,
The necessary contrary:
We bow in gratitude for mediocre lives.
We keep the crow, the rat from the garden.
Like priests, no one mourned when they died.

When they died, we pulled down their cabins.
Then we transported a lawn
That the mad, the hopeless might be buried
— only the strong resisting while strong.
We kept the grass and flowerbeds neatly
But the wilderness wouldn't be put down:

(Children no longer play there
— they stone it —
Nettles stalk the wild grass
Scutch binds the stones together)

Then came the rats.

Epitaph

A colossus on the playing field.
A great man for the crack.
For years he spoke to no one
But turned his sagging back on people.
Head down, he would cycle into town.

Whispers prodded that he be seen to:
'Looked after', slyly said.
Anyone could see
That his head was out of joint.
And he couldn't even hold his lonely pint.

They found him hanging in the barn: dead.
Viciousness turned almost to understanding.
Living alone, never wed . . .
'His uncle did it years before him.
Kind for him,' they said.

('Kind for him': colloquialism meaning 'it was in his nature, in his genes, in his family'.)

A Game of Forty-One

Tonight it's forty-one:
Pay to your right, 10p a man.
Doubles a jink, and play your hand.
If you renege, we'll turn you.

Yes, tonight it's forty-one:
A table for six, any pub in town.
Follow suit, and stand your round.
If you renege, we'll turn you.

Tonight it's forty-one
And tomorrow in the Dáil
Fine Gael and Fianna Fáil
Debate their Bill —

Cos on the television
They're talking of revision
And extension of detention
And extra Special Powers.

So we sit here hour by hour
Getting drunk on special Power:
A game of cards at night now
Costs more and more and more.

And you trump hard on the table,
And you pay up when you're able.
If you don't then you're in trouble
— it's worse than to renege.

Oh, it's always forty-one:
Play your cards at work, at home —
Even sitting on a barstool
They won't let you alone.

Yes, it's always forty-one,
And I'm really in the dumps
For the horsemouth at my elbow
Has just led the Ace of Trumps.

And I'm playing forty-one
And wishing there were some
Other way of spending
A lifetime in this town.

But the poet and the priest
— Beauty and the Beast —
Must all sit down together
And cut this common deck.

And there is no Bill or Bible
But the verdict of the table
And the argument of players
To dispute the point of rule.

So tonight it's forty-one
And tomorrow, next week, next month
And I'm out if I suggest
Another rule.

The Hurt Bird

After playtime
Huddled in the classroom ...

In the yard
Jackdaws peck the ice
While the class guesses
The black birds:

Blackbirds?
(Laughter).

Crows?
Well, yes ...
But jackdaws.
Those are jackdaws.
Why do they peck the ice?

Wonder
Becomes jackdaws' eyes
Rummaging the ice

Till suddenly
At the window opposite

— Oh the bird
The poor bird!

At the shout
The jackdaws fright.

Sir, a robin sir ...
He struck the window
And he fell

And now he's dying
With his legs up
On the ice:

The jackdaws
Will attack it sir.

They will rip its puddings out.

I take the wounded bird,
Deadweight
In my open palm
— no flutter
    no escaping

And lay it
On the floor near heat,
The deadweight
Of the wound
Upon my coat.

Grasping
The ways of pain,
The pain of birds
They cannot name,
The class are curious
But quiet:

They will not frighten
The struggle
Of death and living.

Please sir,
Will he die?

And I
Cannot reply.

Alone
With utter pain

Eyes closed

The little body
Puffed and gasping

Lopsided
Yet upright:

He's alive,
The children whisper
Excited
As if witnessing
His birth.

Would he drink water sir?
Would he eat bread?
Should we feed him?

Lopsided
The hurt bird
With one eye open
To the world
Shits;

He moves
And stumbles.

I move
To the hurt bird:

The beak opens
— for food
    or fight?

I touch
The puffed red breast
With trepid finger;

I spoon water
To the throat:

It splutters.

Children crumb their lunches
Pleading
To lay the broken bread
Within reach of the black head.

The bird
Too hurt to feed
Falls in the valley
Of the coat
And as I help,
It claws
And perches on my finger
Bridging the great divide
Of man and bird.

He hops
From my finger
To the floor

And flutters
Under tables
Under chairs

Till exhausted
He tucks his head
Between wing and breast
Private

Between coat and wall.

The class
Delights in silence
At the sleeping bird.

The bird sir ...
What is it:
A robin?
— Look at the red breast.

But you never see a robin
With a black head.

I tell them
It's a bullfinch
Explaining the colours why;

I answer their questions
From the library.

And the children draw the bullfinch

— With hurt
   And gasp
   And life

— With the fearlessness of pain
   Where the bird will fright

And in the children's pictures
Even black and grey
Are bright.

Getting to Know You

Thomas,
You don't trust me —
I can tell from your trapped eyes.
How can I help you,
My sulky friend?
Tell you I love you?
(That would seem like lies.)
To reach out to touch you
Might offend.

Give you your head:
Watch over
In so far as any human can:
Coax you, with tacit kindness:
Greet you, man to man ...

Yes, Thomas,
I am strong
(But equal) —
And, Thomas,
We are both 'at school':
Both circling round
A common understanding:
Both sniffing at the smile
That sweetens rules.

Today you bounce up to me,
Your eyes the rising sun:

We share your secret story —

Hello!
God bless you,
Tom ...

PATRICK GALVIN

Born in Cork in 1927, Patrick Galvin has had five volumes of poetry published, *Folk Tales for the General* (Raven Arts Press) his most recent. Autobiographies *Song for a Poor Boy* and *Song for a Raggy Boy* were also published by Raven Arts Press. He was Resident Dramatist at the Lyric Theatre, Belfast from 1973 to 1977 and has had plays broadcast on RTE and BBC and staged in Ireland, the UK, Canada and the USA. Resident writer for East Midlands Arts, Nottingham in 1980, his work was recorded in the Library of Congress, Washington DC in 1980/81. A member of Aosdána, he is working on the third volume of an autobiography and a new collection of poetry. He now lives in Cork.

My Father Spoke with Swans

I
Leaning on the parapet
Of the South Gate Bridge
My father spoke with swans
Remembering his days
With the Royal Munster Fusiliers.

India was dawn
The women cool
The sun cradled in his arms.
Sometimes,
When the clouds were wine
He washed his face in the Ganges.

The swans rose from the Lee
And held their wings.

II
Leaning on the mysteries
Of her twilight room

My mother spoke with God
Remembering Pearse
And the breath of Connolly.

Ireland was new
The men tall
The land mirrored their brightness.
Sometimes,
When the eagles called
She walked the roads to Bethlehem.

God opened his eyes
A loss for miracles.

From these two I was born
The Ganges swaying with the Lee
And gunfire rising to a fall.
My mother wore green till she died
My father died with swans.

Only the rivers remain
Slow bleeding.

Nothing is Safe

Nothing is safe anymore.
I wrote a poem last night
And when I woke up this morning
There was no sign of it.

I thought the mice had eaten it
(We're subject to mice in this house)
But then again
Why should they?
Poetry doesn't agree with mice.

Of course,
The present climate being
What it is
Anything may have happened —
A sudden rain storm
During the night
The cold air
Thieving through the window
And the poem dies of pneumonia.

Next time I write a poem
I'll send it to my aunt
Who lives in a madhouse.
She's blind
But she likes the texture of paper.
She holds it in her hand
Crinkles it up
And listens to the sound.

Perhaps
That's all that matters
In the end —
The sound of paper
Screaming in the hand.

Captain Titan

Captain Titan walked on the water
He said he needed the exercise.

At the inquest, Mrs. Titan said that she wasn't too surprised to
hear that her husband had been walking on the water. He was
always doing things like that — especially when he had drink
taken.

The Coroner nodded his head.
He understood perfectly —
The Captain was a seafaring man.

Last year, for example, the Captain had changed into a seagull.
Mrs. Titan had no objections to seagulls. She rather liked them,
really. But the Captain's behaviour as a seagull was quite
outrageous. He insisted on flying in and out of the village church
and screeching for more fish.

The Coroner nodded his head.
He remembered the incident —
The Parish Priest was terrified.

The Captain was arrested for that little escapade and spent three
weeks in jail flapping his wings about and claiming that under
International Law it was illegal to imprison a seagull. Mrs. Titan
knew nothing about International Law, but she was convinced
that the police could arrest anyone for anything — even if he
were a seagull.

The Coroner nodded his head.
He could see the headlines —

'Seagull sues police for wrongful arrest.'

Mrs. Titan said she wasn't a bad wife. She tried hard to be tolerant of the Captain and was sorry now that she hadn't understood him more. After all, there was nothing wrong with being a seagull — and nothing wrong with walking on the water either — if one had a mind to.

The Coroner summed up:
He said
This is a tragic case.
He said
I feel extremely sorry for the widow —
And offered to take her to lunch later
At the nearest seafood restaurant.

ANNE LE MARQUAND HARTIGAN

Anne Le Marquand Hartigan, poet, painter, playwright, has completed four collections of poetry, *Long Tongue* (1982), *Return Single* (1986), *Now is a Moveable Feast* (1991) and a new collection due in 1993. Her plays *Beds* and *La Corbière* were performed at the Dublin Theatre Festival, in 1982 and 1989. She is currently working on a new play, has just completed a book of short stories and will perform a one-woman show in June 1993.

Salt

I would not write a lament for you.
A requiem for you, a song for you,
I would not twine a remembrance for you,
I do not think sweetly of you, of your
Past kindness, past pleasures, past lies.

I am not biding my time for you, not repining
For you, you cause me no more the sleepless nights.
For I have killed you. I have dried you up.
Anger I have for you.
With anger I have washed out pain.
Sweet healing anger opening my eyes on you.
Seeing you, without the love blur in them.
Tears now pillars of salt.

Could call curses on you, spit on you,
Laugh at you, but I just smile at you,
Leave you alone. Climbed free of you
Away from the power of you the hold of you
The grip of you the hurt of you from
Feeding the need of you, filling you.

Bringing gifts to you. Bringing strengths
To you. I turn my power on you,
I shine that fierce light on you, you cannot
Move or run, Caught in my full beam
Only I can unleash this moving thing.
You cannot understand it you cannot know it
But you can feel it under your brain;
Rabbit you, caught in my glare.

Clear of you, clean of you
Swept of you, no more bereft of you,
My kisses not for you
No words for you
No sweet looks for you
No look over my shoulder for you.
Turn my heel on you, my back to you.
I have no lack of you. It is you
That is to be pitied now.

from 'Winter the Man',
the last section in *Now is a Moveable Feast*

Auctioneer:
> This gentleman's residence is very secluded;
> would suit executive, with expansive views,
> is near all amenities of town and country,
> river and sea ....

Are you coming by night

by water
by holocaust
by motor car or
by accident?

Are you coming?

Dressed in royal garments
anointed with chrism
with blessings
by fire
with brimstone
with hair lacquer.

Are you coming?

Often or now
or not now or never
or tomorrow or
the Wednesday after
next?

The old bull lay dying
but they

kept their distance
for fear of a last twist of that
mighty head.

The rest
fled,

scurrying and disorderly
bickering for inheritance.

The old bull
lay in the dust.

They kept watch,
waiting,
for the timekeeper.

This space from morning to evening
is longer than ever
than this ever
or ever after.

The children,
two daughters
one son,

crept closer,

brought water,
for the old bull lay
dying.

They had their duty
and knew there
were things that must

things they had to face
and the space between now
and then must be filled

carefully
with ritual.

The candles lighted.

Because they could now
see clearer than ever before,

each flame
a new opening
in the dark.

Giving a place
to the space in the head.

The old bull lay dying.
His black shoulders
his pulse marking
tickering tickering.

The bull alone on a circle of sand.

Red from his nostrils
gold of his horns
move as a blessing.

What is he minding
in that deep cranium,
wounds in the mind
that have inward bled?

The days of dominion
when a stamp of his hooves
a lowering head
brought the tribe to its knees:

now the tongue lodged
and lead.

      Clasping of fingers
      dropping of eyes
      why are we kneeling?

'He is one of the old ones'
the Timekeeper said.

'Belonging to times that
are not now.'

His thumb pressed
the stop-watch

Dead.

The black bull lay still

the clan scattered
and fled.

MICHAEL D. HIGGINS

Michael D. Higgins was born in Limerick city and reared in Co Clare. He has been a lecturer in Political Science and Sociology at UCG, a Senator, Dáil Deputy and is currently Minister for Arts, Culture and the Gaeltacht. His first collection *Betrayal* was published by Salmon; his second, *Season of Fire*, by Brandon.

The Betrayal

A Poem for My Father

This man is seriously ill,
The doctor had said a week before,
Calling for a wheelchair.
It was
After they rang me
To come down
And persuade you
To go in to hospital,
Condemned to remember your eyes
As they met mine in that moment
Before they wheeled you away.
It was one of my final tasks
To persuade you to go in,
A Judas chosen not by Apostles
But by others more broken;
And I was, in part,
Relieved when they wheeled you from me,
Down that corridor, confused,
Without a backward glance
And when I had done it,
I cried, out on the road,
Hitching a lift to Galway and away

From the trouble of your
Cantankerous old age
And rage too,
At all that had in recent years
Befallen you.

All week I waited to visit you
But when I called, you had been moved
To where those dying too slowly
Were sent,
A poorhouse, no longer known by that name,
But in the liberated era of Lemass,
Given a saint's name, 'St. Joseph's'.
Was he Christ's father,
Patron saint of the Worker,
The mad choice of some pietistic politician?
You never cared.

Nor did you speak too much.
You had broken an attendant's glasses,
The holy nurse told me,
When you were admitted.
Your father is a very difficult man,
As you must know.
And Social Welfare is slow
And if you would pay for the glasses,
I would appreciate it.
It was 1964, just after optical benefit
Was rejected by De Valera's cabinet for poorer classes
In his Republic, who could not afford,
As he did
to travel to Zurich
For their regular tests and their
Rimless glasses.

It was decades earlier
You had brought me to see him
Pass through Newmarket-on-Fergus
As the brass and reed band struck up,
Cheeks red and distended to the point
Where a child's wonder was as to whether
They would burst as they blew
Their trombones.
The Sacred Heart Procession and De Valera,
You told me, were the only occasions
When their instruments were taken
From the rusting, galvanised shed
Where they stored them in anticipation
Of the requirements of Church and State.

Long before that, you had slept,
In ditches and dug-outs,
Prayed in terror at ambushes
With others who later debated
Whether De Valera was lucky or brilliant
In getting the British to remember
That he was an American.
And that debate had not lasted long
In detention camps in Newbridge
And the Curragh, where mattresses were burned,
As the gombeens decided that the new State
Was a good thing,
Even for business.

In the dining-room of St. Joseph's
The potatoes were left in the middle of the table
In a dish, towards which
You and many other Republicans
Stretched feeble hands that shook.
Your eyes were bent as you peeled

With the long thumb-nail I had often watched
Scrape a pattern on the leather you had toughened
    for my shoes,
Your eyes when you looked at me
Were a thousand miles away,
Now totally broken,
Unlike those times even
Of rejection, when you went at sixty
For jobs you never got,
Too frail to load vans, or manage
The demands of selling.
And I remember
When you came back to me,
Your regular companion of such occasions,
And said, They think that I'm too old
For the job. I said I was fifty-eight
But they knew that I was past sixty.

A body ready for transportation,
Fit only for a coffin, that made you
Too awkward
For death at home.
The shame of a coffin exit
Through a window sent you here,
Where my mother told me you asked
Only for her to place her cool hand
Under your neck.
And I was there when they asked
Would they give you a Republican funeral,
In that month when you died,
Between the end of the First Programme for
    Economic Expansion
And the Second.

I look at your photo now,
Taken in the beginning of bad days,
With your surviving mates
In Limerick.
Your face haunts me as do these memories;
And all these things have been scraped
In my heart,
And I can never hope to forget
What was, after all,
A betrayal.

RITA ANN HIGGINS

Poet and playwright Rita Ann Higgins lives in Galway. Among her publications are *Goddess on the Mervue Bus* (Salmon Publishing 1986), *Witch in the Bushes* (Salmon Publishing 1988) and *Philomena's Revenge* (Salmon Publishing 1992). In 1986 she received a writing bursary from the Arts Council.

Poetry Doesn't Pay

People keep telling me
Your poems, you know,
you've really got something there,
I mean really.

When the rent man calls, I go
down on my knees, and through
the conscience box I tell him.

This is somebody speaking,
short distance, did you know
I have something here with my poems?
People keep telling me.

'All I want is fourteen pounds
and ten pence, hold the poesy.'

But you don't realise
I've got something here.

'If you don't come across
with fourteen pounds and ten pence soon
you'll have something at the side of the road,
made colourful by a little snow.'

But.

'But nothing,
you can't pay me in poems or prayers
or with your husband's jokes,
or with photographs of your children
in lucky lemon sweaters
hand-made by your dead Grand Aunt
who had amnesia and the croup.

'I'm from the Corporation,
what do we know or care about poesy,
much less grand amnostic dead aunts.'

But people keep telling me.

'They lie.

'If you don't have fourteen pounds
and ten pence, you have nothing
but the light of the penurious moon.'

Mona

Mona doesn't die here
anymore, she lives
in a house at the back
of her mind.

Some place small,
cosy and warm,
fully detached,

a single storey,
with no gable ending,
a high wall
but no door.

Away from
tenants' associations,
rent man's,
poor man's,
light bills,
heavy bills,
free newspapers,
and six-year-old perpetrators on skates.

When she was here
she was afraid
of salutations,
candied appreciations,
of tendon squeezing
politicians
who didn't care.

In supermarkets
she was tricked by
pennies off here,
free holidays over there,
buy three and get
anxiety for nothing.

She was a coupon saver,
she saved them
but they never saved her.

Mona doesn't die there
anymore, she lives

in a shed at the back
of her house.

Some place small,
cosy and warm,
a high wall
but no door.

The Did-You-Come-Yets of the Western World

When he says to you:
You look so beautiful
you smell so nice —
how I've missed you —
and did not come yet?

It means nothing,
and he is smaller
than a mouse's fart.

Don't listen to him ...
Go to Annaghdown Pier
with your father's rod.
Don't necessarily hold out
for the biggest one;
oftentimes the biggest ones
are the smallest in the end.

Bring them all home,
but not together.
One by one is the trick;
avoid red herrings and scandal.

Maybe you could take two
on the shortest day of the year.
Time is the cheater here
not you, so don't worry.

Many will bite the usual bait:
They will talk their slippery way
through fine clothes and expensive perfume,
fishing up your independence.

These are,
The did-you-come-yets of the western world,
the feather and fin rufflers.
Pity for them they have no wisdom.

Others will bite at any bait.
Maggot, suspender, or dead worm.
Throw them to the sharks.

In time one will crawl
out from under thigh-land.
Although drowning he will say,

'Woman I am terrified, why is the house shaking?'

And you'll know he's the one.

FRED JOHNSTON

Born in Belfast in 1951, Fred Johnston has worked as a professional journalist for some years. Now living in Galway, he has also lived in Algeria and Spain. He received a Hennessy Literary Award in 1972 and an Arts Council Literary Bursary in 1988. A founder of the Irish Writers Co-op, he initiated Cúirt, Galway's annual poetry festival, in 1986. He has had a novel, three collections and a cassette of poems published. He has reviewed for the *Sunday Times*, the *Irish Times*, *Poetry Ireland*, *Books Ireland* and the *Irish University Review*.

Letter to a Disciple
(from the Arabic of Al-Ghazali, 1107)

Be under no illusions,
you owe it to yourself to stay clear
whenever you can of the dubious patronage
of those who say they have a hand in the
pocket to help you out in times of difficulty

Make a wide path around them and those
who doff their caps to them and laugh
even when they don't understand their jokes;
there's nothing in it for you but humiliation
and disappointment

Now and then you may find you have no
choice, for one reason or another, but
to rub shoulders with this lot: but you
are under no obligation to indulge them
or make them feel you owe them something

They would laugh up their sleeves at you
if they got the chance, and in the end
you can only hurt yourself.

Heartlands

The winter of my fourteenth year
behind the fenced firs, near the
road, someone out walking found
a foetus, parcelled, anonymous

it created monstrous legends,
local libels which stuck then
peeled away with time
the first child of the North

had not yet been shot dead.
Years later, the fenced firs gone,
a rude box of apartments driven
there like the bite of a giant tooth,

dead kids no longer cause a scandal,
no longer excite; I have a child
of my own, born up there in the
old heartlands, and she

does not remember —
as her drenched head appeared,
out in the Emergency bay an ambulance
screamed and soldiers' boots

banged up the polished parquet
hallways with the steady rehearsed
tattoo of men sure of their business:
we've come a very long way.

For Emma

Your name has a biblical ring
in this city of biblethumpers and Old
Testament cruelties
two syllables singing like a bell

I'd spray your name and mine on a
gable-end, scratch our initials in
a 'phone-box, as good as a fire on the
Cave Hill for the whole city to see

child of the dustbin territories, their
tinlid tattoo entered your ears at birth
echoes in the anteroom of the heart
even now, like the memory of a first kiss

you've worn it well, Emma,
the handed-down tattery shawl of tribal
suffering
you will never turn it into a flag

or hide beneath it. No, it's in your
voice, the frank shape of your mouth
they have painted no slogans on any wall
in our town to describe how you feel

at all times beauty is more precious
than their violence, the men who have made
your dreams unsafe
squalid ghosts, fleshy myths

you must never wring your hands
for them. I would step through the wire
take your poems and your wonder at the
world and make a pagan music

and watch you dance
your way through their peace-lines and
their concrete bunkers
liberty is always a woman

your sing-song sarcasm reminds me of
the song they stole from us
I feel the weight of the loss of what
I once was, of what you are still

in this city of pious bell-ringers
and hymns raised up in honour of murder
your full clear note sounds loudest
and breaks the heart.

We are Rivers, Frozen

There is a notion that time has passed
a considerable length of time
and that we have become two persons
each quite changed and grown wiser

there is a strict myth to be observed
how we've grown to understandings
mutual affections but no real concern
how we've learned to take it on the chin

and also there is what the others say
was best, and it is easy to obey
take orders when the heart is numb:
there is the ritual of passing by

I have taken all I can from the high-
priests of consolation and sacrifice:
be firm, they said, leaving me alone
and losing hold

I have waited as long as I dare for
some evidence that what we shared is
remembered and may be revived: this
is almost a religion, the need of faith

blinds all other concerns. This is
our winter and we are rivers, frozen —
too much wisdom has consumed the flame
when I was innocent there was magic in your name.

NAN JOYCE

Nan Joyce was born in 1940 in Tipperary, and learned her letters from her mother. An activist for Travellers' rights, she has stood for election to Dáil Éireann as a Travellers' candidate. She is an inspired speaker and singer, and lives in Tallaght.

The Wild Trabler

The wild trabler the wild
trabler is a man dat fit when he is drunk
and ol ws shoten dat pepel tinkes he is ful of heat
But no gust a man dat life left be hind
a man hum never had a chanc in life since he wos born
on wonte out cast in hes on cuntrey senc he was a child
he was regetd leven wild lick the birds
ben hunted lick a wild anamel Pepel snar at hem
and a fard of hem Lif never brot hem aney hapnes
he corses the day he wos boorn He som times ask God
why he was put on ert he is a on happy man hum never had
a tru frend den he turns to the onley frend
he has, the frend dat makes hem laf and cry and happy
for whil. A frend dat wil breng hem tloser to det.
Dis a wild man

The Wild Traveller

The Wild Traveller. The wild traveller
is a man that fights when he is drunk
and always shouting, that people think
he is full of hate. But no,
Just a man that life left behind
A man who never had a chance in life
Since he was born. Unwanted, outcast
In his own country since he was a child
He was rejected, living wild like the birds
Being hunted like a wild animal.
People snarl at him and are afraid of him.
Life never brought him any happiness.
He curses the day he was born.
He sometimes asks God why he was put on earth.
He is an unhappy man who never had a true friend
Then he turns to the only friend he has. The friend
That makes him laugh and cry and happy for a while
A friend that will bring him closer to death.
This is a wild man.

Leland Bardwell

ANNE KENNEDY

Anne Kennedy is a writer, radio broadcaster and photographer. She leads writers' workshops for the Galway Arts Centre and Barna VEC. Her work has been published in Ireland and America.

---

from *Buck Mountain Poems*

1.
The road to Buck Mountain
ends at my cabin.
From the cliff it appears
to travel underwater and surface
as the lights that fly up the ski run
above Vancouver.
Last night my road sliced the sky
all the way to the Arctic;
my neighbour called it the Northern Lights.

4.
After a quarrel
lying on a stone above Buck Bay
I am surrounded by otters
tossing flounders, joyous sport.
They don't see me lying there
still as the land curve
that vanishes north.
I long to slip in with them
and float among the reeds.

5.
In search of trout
I walk up a steep logging trail.
The spring air spins out a frail heat.

Halfway up Buck Mountain I discover a pond
and catch dinner.
When my neighbour later boasts
he owns my hidden pond,
'man-made and routinely stocked,'
imagine my dismay.

8.
The blackberries we bring down in pails
from Buck Mountain have caught
part of the summer;
leaves and drowned wasps tumble
into the enamel colander
to be washed away in a river of juice.
All through the short days of winter
we will spoon this wild fruit
from sky-blue jars.

9.
The summer visitors have all left the island;
we gather rosehips around their empty cabins.
The North Shore is ours again
and no one comes down the road
without reason.
Even the mailboxes look abandoned
except ours,
which creaks when I open it
in the cold morning air.

11.
A lightning storm knocks out the power
so I bathe by candlelight;
a bowl of oranges
glows with an oily luminescence
on a Persian tin tray.
No need to pull the curtains,

who would call by
on such a wild night?

16.

The pond at the foot of Buck Mountain has frozen
      over
trapping two mallards in a sheet of ice.
Knowing the neighbour's pups will venture out
and kill them for sport,
we risk the ice in our heavy clothes
and bring the helpless ducks
back to the cabin to thaw.
Releasing them later at the lake,
they are lost in a cloud of birds.

18.

Except in high summer
it takes a fool to live on Buck Mountain;
smoke no longer rises from the chimneys
and frost splits the alders.
Only the generous moon
throwing a thousand fractured stars
into the frozen rain barrel
breaks the gloomy spell.

20.

On a morning when our breath hangs between us
I say goodbye to my neighbour.
We are leaving Buck Mountain
for a sun-swept farm on another island.
Warming his hands over the glowing stove,
he offers to buy back the cabin
confessing he always knew the pipes would freeze
and that for months
we would barely glimpse
The sun.

JEROME KIELY

Born in Kinsale, Co Cork in 1925, Jerome Kiely was ordained a priest in 1950. At present he is parish priest of Aughadown in West Cork. He has written two collections of poetry, *The Griffon Sings* (1966) and *Yesterdays of the Heart* (1989), and two prose books, *Seven Year Island* (1969) and *Isle of the Blest* (1993). Currently working on a long poem, *World with an End*, his interests include sports cars, wildlife, travel and sailing.

The Swallows are Behind Schedule

I wanted them to come to-day.
Why didn't they?
The wind was south
with insect banquets north of mouth.
Always on April twentieth
I got the news of winter's death:
the sickly spring revived,
swallows arrived.
Sunday too and it would have been meet
for swallows to have praised their Lord with fleet
and skilful ringarounding of the spire
of Goleen church, something far higher
than all the thoughts we raised, prayers of request,
pigmy things or six feet two at best.
If they had come, if it had come to pass
I could have named it Feast of Swallowmas.

But no, when I looked out my window, not
a swallow could I see attempt to dot
the steeple's letter I in fun
or, purposeful as nun,
to tie a bow about the cross,

grace the ribbon, speed the gloss.
I asked the altarboys if they had seen
them yet, and Dermot Sheehan
said yes, up in Kilbrown
the weight of them would bring the wires down.

Invention is a youngster's poetry:
I liked his phrase but it was clear to me
it was last autumn's freeze he saw
not this year's thaw.
And Vincent Goggin's fibs were sparrows
and not the flying armoury of arrows
shot from Norman France to here
piercing the primeval air.

So after Mass I went to look for them
in two spots they are fond of: first, the glen
road from Kealfada to Dreenane where they
like to propel themselves on wires all day,
wires of their own devising. I must add:
to them man's readymades look restrictive, bad
for business — and up and down they zing
like Lambourne cups that bring
your change from countinghouse to floor
in some uncommon old department store.
The shop was shut, they weren't there.

So on with me again to where
the tumbling hills of Letter break
their fall in Lissigriffin lake.
That's where I saw them first last year
doing a test run of their scooping gear:
the lead plane swooped and took a sample,
the squadron followed its example,
they buzzed the waves, zigzagged away

eluding all the tracers of the spray,
then made three low reconnaissancing runs
above the proud armada of the swans
painted a saucy white — such arrogance! —
anachronisms near the U-boat cormorants.
All summer tall the swallows kept control;
threat in their sweptback wings, the lake patrol
never relaxed; skythreading to skytear
they flew their course refuelling in midair.
But no such luck for eyes to-day:
the dreams crashlanded on the way.

So I came back the road frustrated;
but this neuralgia is now all but abated
and not because the energetic birds
have shaped and fuselaged these building words:
the reason is as I write this
I realise how beautiful a swallow is
and nothing so accomplished could demean
itself to be a servant of routine,
and when it takes off from a land afar
its destination is no printed calendar.

Wreath on a Farmer's Coffin

The flowers in their funeral wreath
spoke far too loud like drunkards in their pub —
familiar breed —
and smelt of alcohol and urban greed.

The names attached were of a pair
who under licence slaked the dead man's thirst;
alternately they were
the precise verdict of a coroner.

Beast after beast, field after field
the farmer tossed across their counter, till
all that was left to yield
was wreckage that the bodypaint concealed.

Their floor was patterned with the marks
his bullocks left; behind their softskinned smiles
hard bones were clerks;
their till's mouth opened like a killer shark's.

'He'll never come to any harm'
they said, but came the day his empty stool
leapt in alarm.
His corpse dammed up the effluent of his farm.

They brought their wreath, their signed receipt,
and left it on the coffin in the church
(where God brooks no deceit)
where all who doubted love could witness it

at Requiem Mass; and undismayed
transformed their victim's coffin to a float
in a parade
with their advertisement right vividly displayed.

The Valiant Woman

They were as blunt as boots.
They told the woman that her son was dead.
Dead.
The half door of the summer shut,
the dresser emptied.
Then they listed the first cousins of the fact:
stretched he was
on the floor of the cliff
north of the cabhlach.
Was he broken like a crab? she asked.
No, it wasn't any fall he got:
they found him in the swimming hole
sound as a pealed
potato in a pot.
They would bring him back to her
but first they needed rope
to pull him up the cliff.
You'll do no such a thing,
he's not a sack of meal,
she said.

She ran before them to the cliff
through pounding fields,
and crouching on her heels
slid down the swimmers' gully, fast
as children down a playground chute,
the menfolk following, one by one,
like sailors out of rigging, slow,
on apprehensive limbs.
She saw two men standing by the body
like farmers on a slack fair day,

detached, knowing they won't buy.
They had him habited in Christian brown,
a piece of sailcloth they had wound
about his slim unseasoned spar.
She rolled him out of it
as if it was shaking out a reef she was
and looked at what the Lord had left her,
a washed corpse.

Without a word, a tear,
or helpless helping hand
she bent to lift her drowned son up,
and hunchbacked by inheritance
she bounded up the gully track
as human never should.
The white youth seemed an angel lifting
the woman's body up the cliff:
those who were there and saw it said
the dead one looked like the living
and the living looked like the dead.
She steadied like a cromlech at the top,
then went her sacred way
between the faceless neighbours, standing stones,
back along the blindness to the house.
Behind her moved the men like beads
singly like beads, like small black beads
of the Lady Rosary stretched out,
herself in front carrying the mortal cross.
She shut the door upon them all
to be alone,
alone with her sorrow and her son.

JESSIE LENDENNIE

Born in Arkansas, USA in 1946 and educated in King's College, London, Jessie Lendennie has lived in Galway since 1981. A founding editor of *The Salmon* journal (1981) and co-founder of Salmon Publishing (1985), she has devoted all her energies since 1986 to establishing Salmon Publishing as a major poetry publisher. Salmon recently joined the Poolbeg Group, and this will allow her more time for her own writing.

---

from *Daughter*

She had no black dress. How would she have a dress her mother had not bought her? In the room her mother's clothes hung ... she touched them, knew them as alive; house dress, work dress ... In the room Emma sat, hiding under her mother's dresses, under the clothes of no one, under a lingering smell.

And her mother's mother, her mother's sisters spoke around her; distant sounds growing more faint. She clasped the sounds as buoys in the ocean, markers of survival ... was she dead? Would she be dead if she could no longer hear the sounds? Was her mother dead ... dead? They said it, and she hated the house full of people; ghosts in a hollow rain, ghosts in a sunlight rain.

She touched her mother's dress, red orange stripe, and her mother undressed for bed, pulled the dress over her head, folded it ... and the pain was ageless ... timeless.

***

How could she know there would be no forgetting? That she would always remember ... that this was her life, and

when they said, 'She's grown out of it ... ' they were
wrong, wrong.

***

*In the East the sea rose, wave against wave, climbing cliffs no
longer visible.*

*She stirred in her sleep, falling downwards with the flow between
rain and sea.*

*The mist hung beyond daylight, and the sounds were of a night
not yet over.*

*She woke from a dream of running, running. She lay still and
knew she could not move. The blanket covering her was heavy,
heavy as her breath in the still air.*

***

'Mama, I'm hungry.'
Emma's mother gripped the shirt she was mending.
'Mama, I'm hungry.'
Emma came up to the porch and stood at the bottom step.
Still her mother did not answer.
'I don't have nobody to play with.' She flopped on the
step and the dog came close.
'I'll play with you.' Her mother's smile was tired.
Emma stuck her chin forcefully into muddy palms and
turned away.

***

*She lay still and thought the sounds she heard were the
beginnings of comfort. Thought she could feel the sea on the
wind; the fall, falling of the waves. Wind sails riding the horizon.
The cold wash of the ocean against the walls of her small room.*

***

Rows upon rows of cotton plants in the heat. Emma
watched the pickers moving along the rows, filling their
long trailing sacks. She rode the end of her mother's
cotton-sack, making patterns with her fingers in the dust.
She daydreamed lazily as the sack grew softer and her
mother's pace slowed. She saw her sister running
awkwardly behind them, heard her brothers arguing,
and above her, her mother's mild voice.

***

In the darkness she imagined the silence at the centre of the wind.
Hoped for the sound of rain; counted hours, years. Saw the
morning path leading away between the cliffs.

***

'Emma, Emma, look here, Daddy brought you
somethin'.'
Emma opened her eyes slowly, the smell of her father
enveloped her. It was dark and he was outlined by the
light from the hall, holding his hand forward. She sat up.
The parakeet was skinny, a faded blue-green, dying. She
took it from him. It lay on her outstretched palms.

'I won it for you, at the fair.' Her father swayed, and she
felt suddenly frightened.
She felt the dead weight of the bird; looked past her
father, saw her mother hesitating in the doorway.

***

And she knew the haunted dark; the shadows falling from the sky.
Falling like the end of a nightmare, black as silence, cold as white
light when the fog lifts on a winter day.

***

'And this ticket is for my daughter,' Emma's mother
smiled at the ticket collector.
Blytheville, Arkansas to Hawthorne, California ... and
what in between?
Hours on the Salt Lake of Utah, more snow than she
could imagine in Denver. Emma loved the sounds, the
names ... California ... and now daughter.
Daughter, daughter, daughter, she repeated the word.
Daughter, daughter, daughter ... a train sound through
the night.

***

She lay still and the darkness lay with her.

*In the morning she would go along the beach, below the cliffs,
into the mist.*

*In the morning there would be boats with red sails, out early on
a fair wind.*

***

Emma's mother was dying.
'Cancer,' her aunts whispered, 'Cancer.'
Emma did not know the word. Could not stay in the
house with the whispering. She bit her lip, stood in the
doorway looking out.

***

*She dreamed of the storm as it raged above the cliffs, and the
storm kept the sunlight from her; it ran above and away from her,
returned to her, alone and dreaming.*

***

'Your Mama died this afternoon.' Her father did not
look at her.

***

Through the blur of California pink, yellow skies Emma
felt the sun set. Walked tidy streets, smelled figs rotting in
alleyways, heard lawn sprinklers under a blank sun on
white stucco.

She thought she heard the wind as she once had ...
through the grass, rising in the poplar trees; a rushing
wind in a pale spring time. She would not cry.

***

Rough sway sweep of trees, scrape of branches, ink
scratches across the sky; the curving sidewalk cracked
with ice coloured like mud, rainbow patterns in spilt
gasoline. Walk, walking a jagged crack refined with grass
under trees like stars grown wild ... and what are those
things? Starlight, starbright, first star I see ... the biggest
that means closest; but that was summer and this was
spring, April ...

***

'Emma, your Mama said ... '

Across the Bay ... a sailboat on a fine day,
a sail now white, now black ...

and the child said, 'If you love me, take me with you.'

JOHN LIDDY

Born in Youghal in Co Cork in 1954, John Liddy grew up and was educated in Limerick. He has read and lectured widely in Ireland, the USA, Serbia, Spain and Brittany. He has had two collections of poetry published, *Boundaries* (1975) and *The Angling Cot* (1991) with poems translated into Serbo-Croat, Breton-French and Spanish. He is co-editor of *The Stony Thursday Book/ Cuaderro de Madrid*. He now lives and works in Madrid.

Words for Samuel Beckett

I read on.
Understanding less.
Yet I could not leave you.
Each word brought
Me to the next.

Then days of brooding.
Of difficulty.
Until little by little
I saw the word complete.
Felt as my own heartbeat.

I read on.
The same problem.
But always the word
Keeping me in touch.

Out of such ignorance
I learned much.

Good Things

for Joe Malone

I am consoled by the love of things.
Things quiet and gentle for the eye
To rest on. For thought to equal
Itself out again. Things ordinary
And simple. Like the casual sweep
Of a brush or the feel of cloth
Between finger and thumb.
Things momentary and accidental.
The way a sleeping wasp might turn
In a hollow knot of wood. Good
Things found on street and floor:
Acorn, feather, colourful string.
Things that get lost in the pile up
Of things huge and bewildering.

Southern Comfort

In '69 it was different.
Something had to be done.
So we turned up our television sets
And replaced the game of 45
With talk of war.
But it never happened
At least not in the South.
So we grew careless
With the daily atrocities
And took to the cards again.

Then the bombs went off
In Dublin, Galway, Limerick
And Killarney.
So we beat our knuckles
On counters of self pity
And swore to join 'the boys'.
We were angrily suspicious
And talked about reprisals.
When the damage and the dead
Were known we sat around
The pulpit and shaped
Our prayers like bullets.

Now we refer to the killing
As 'the troubles'.
We are thankful to God
For the Sunday morning chat,
The quiet pathway home from the pub.
We look forward to the annual
Dinner dance, are stirred
By the occasional public debate.

But we know what it means
To be a majority.
We know how to tip our caps
At our confessors
Who would forgive us anything.

JOAN Mc BREEN

Joan Mc Breen is from Sligo but now lives in Tuam, Co Galway. She is a primary teacher. Her poetry has been widely published in Ireland, the USA and Canada. *The Wind Beyond the Wall,* her first collection, was published by Story Line Press, USA in 1990. She has recently completed a second collection.

Valkenswaard

Poppies and corn flowers lit
the yellow fields near Valkenswaard
and I felt my child's skin warm
under my fingers as he slept

in the crook of my arms
and the shadows stretched
across the brown wooden floor
under his white bed

when I shook sand
from his scuffed shoes
and heard the whisper of his breath
in the dark room

before moths were drawn
to the candle flaming
over the beer and the bread
on the platter between us

and we crept to bed almost
without remembering
to put his small blue flowers
in the stone water jug on his window sill.

Woman in Winter

I am a woman in my green kitchen, in winter.

When you come in from the street,
do you see how elegantly
my table is set,
how the chrysanthemums blaze
in the fine glass vase
on the window sill?

I am sitting here waiting
for you to stop talking
about last night's storms.

My apron is hanging
on the back of the chair,
my hands are resting
on the table but
at any moment,
they might lift that vase
and hurl it onto
the brown tiled floor.

The Woman in the Yellow Dress

There was nobody in the field,
so she went in
through the gate
in her yellow dress,
her stomach in a knot,

148

and she lay down
in the wet grass, the first
to leave the shape
of a body there.

She opened her dress
because there was nobody
to see her and she slept
while the whole of the summer
hummed around her
and she dreamed
of no wretched weather.

Waking, she shook her hair free
from the thick pins that tightened
it in a coil
at the back of her neck
and for a time
the grass stopped growing
where she lay, and she forgot
his voice, his arms, until

he approached her
with wolves on his shoulders.
She braided her hair
and buttoned her dress.
Taking the wolves from him
into her arms she followed
him out through the gate
with her heart full of grey snow.

This Moon, These Stars

Something is changing.
There is a September stillness in the garden.

We have woken in this bed for years.
You have followed me into my poems,
my dreams, my past, to places I scarcely
know of myself.

I called one evening
from our back doorstep. 'Look,' I said,
'look at this moon.' We stood there
in silence, not touching, not knowing
what to say.

We have been together many days, many nights.
These stars have come out
over us again and again.

Here is the life we are living,
not on a windswept beach, not in vast
city streets, not in a strange country
but here, where we have chosen to be.

I look at myself in the glass, at the woman
I am.

I think of our days, our years running on
into each other.

What will we say,
what will we know.

Separate, together,
will we find the right way, the dream
neither of us can explain.

I pull the living room curtains together.
The garden is around us,
still above us are the stars,
light and indestructible.

STEVE Mac DONOGH

Born in Dublin, Steve Mac Donogh has lived since 1982 in Dingle where he is editorial director of Brandon Book Publishers. His poetry has been appearing in magazines in the USA, Britain and Ireland since the '60s and he is the author of three collections of poetry, a folklore study and a local history.

By Dingle Bay and Blasket Sound

In Ballyferriter in Corca Dhuibhne
the Three Sisters rear their heads to look
out over the endless expanse of the sea.
In Ballyferriter in Corca Dhuibhne
cohorts of German boy scouts
shade their eyes towards Atlantic sunset;
beside them a gaggle of girls from Dublin
pile into the bus for the Dún an Óir.
No one grows up in Ballyferriter
without having one eye on the horizon
where sky meets sea and clouds roll in.
No one looks at the outline of the 'Dead Man';
no one watches the light change in the west
of an evening that moves from blue to yellow,
from yellow to gold, to pink, red and purple;
no one watches or looks without knowing
that on the far distant shore of the ocean
lies a new destination, a life and a home
in a place that will never be home.
In Daniel Keane's a Corkman plays fiddle,
a Yank talks folklore and a Dub sings;
at the bar three local men in their sixties,
their eyes sinking misty into pints.
There are Spaniards in the Blasket Sound,

seized by the great mouth of the sea
from ships of the Armada;
Blasket and mainland fishermen too,
pulled to death before their time.
And now it is the air that plucks
the young of Ballyferriter
not to death but to exile
from the gateways of farewell
at Shannon, Cork and Dublin.
No one grows up in Ballyferriter
without having one eye on the horizon,
or an ear to the phone for news from beyond
from sisters, brothers, friends ...
And in the lands of opportunity
young emigrants dream
of becoming anything they wish,
yet know the reality of the possible.
But 'home,' they say, 'is the only place
you can just be yourself.'
Home is the deep and healing well
to which they return; and here
they pay the round and dance
like pilgrims at an old pattern.
Few see the reasons for their exile,
few want to know, it being enough
to learn a new place in a new world.
At home it is only brochures
and bureaucrats that brag
about the wonders of deep ploughs;
the rest register vegetables
rotting on the dump or ploughed back,
register an industry of excuses
for management expenses.
The confident promontory forts
express a proud, developed past,

but their ruins watch over
seas whose produce is stolen
and fields where buachalláin buí
is the only crop.
The people of Duibhne are scattering
while wide-boys and apparatchiks
bray like satisfied donkeys,
reaping funds in the name
of heritage and co-operation.
Language is turned on its head:
money gives power to liars,
makes fools of true women and men.
No one grows up in Ballyferriter
without having one eye on the horizon
where sky meets sea and clouds roll in.

MÁIRE Mhac an tSAOI

Poet and scholar, Máire Mhac an tSaoi writes principally in the Irish language. She is a former member of the Irish foreign service, married to Conor Cruise O'Brien and has two adopted children.

Ceathrúintí Mháire Ní Ógáin

I

Ach a mbead gafa as an líon so —
Is nár lige Dia gur fada san —
Béidir go bhfónfaidh cuimhneamh
Ar a bhfuaireas de shuaimhneas id bhaclainn.

Nuair a bheidh ar mo chumas guíochtaint,
Comaoine is éisteacht Aifrinn,
Cé déarfaidh ansan nach cuí dhom
Ar 'shonsa is ar mo shon féin achaine?

Ach comhairle idir dhá linn duit,
Ná téir ródhílis in achrann,
Mar go bhfuilimse meáite ar scaoileadh
Pé cuibhrinn a snaidhmfear eadrainn.

II

Beagbheann ar amhras daoine,
Beagbheann ar chros na sagart,
Ar gach ní ach a bheith sínte
Idir tú agus falla —

Neamhshuím liom fuacht na hoíche,
Neamhshuím liom scríb is fearthainn,
Sa domhan cúng rúin teolaí seo
Ná téann thar fhaobhar na leapan —

Ar a bhfuil romhainn ní smaoinfeam,
Ar a bhfuil déanta cheana,
Linne an uain, a chroí istigh,
Is mairfidh sí go maidin.

III

Achar bliana atáim
Ag luí farat id chlúid,
Deacair anois a rá
Cad leis a raibh mo shúil!

Ghabhais de chosaibh i gcion
A tugadh chomh fial ar dtúis,
Gan aithint féin féd throigh
Fulag na feola a bhrúigh!

Is fós tá an creat umhal
Ar mhaithe le seanagheallúint,
Ach ó thost cantain an chroí
Tránn áthas na bpléisiúr.

IV

Tá naí an éada ag deol mo chí'se
Is mé ag tál air de ló is d'oíche;
An gárlach gránna ag cur na bhfiacal,
Is de nimh a ghreama mo chuisle líonta.

A ghrá, ná maireadh an trú beag eadrainn,
Is a fholláine, shláine a bhí ár n-aithne;
Barántas cnis a chloígh lem chneas airsin,
Is séala láimhe a raibh gach cead aici.

Féach nach meáite mé ar chion a shéanadh,
Cé gur sháigh an t-amhras go doimhin a phréa'cha;

Ar láir dhea-tharraic ná déan éigean,
Is díolfaidh sí an comhar leat ina séasúr féinig.

V

Is éachtach an rud í an phian,
Mar chaitheann an cliabh,
Is ná tugann faoiseamh ná spás
Ná sánas de ló ná d'oích' —

An té atá i bpéin mar táim
Ní raibh uaigneach ná ina aonar riamh,
Ach ag iompar cuileachtan de shíor
Mar bhean gin féna coim.

VI

'Ní chodlaím ist oíche' —
Beag an rá, ach an bhfionnfar
        choíche
Ar shúile oscailte
Ualach na hoíche?

Fada liom anocht!
Do bhí ann oíche
Nárbh fhada faratsa —
Dá leomhfainn cuimhneamh.

Go deimhin níor dheacair san,
An ród a d'fhillfinn —
Dá mba cheadaithe
Tar éis aithrí ann.

Luí chun suilt
Is éirí chun aoibhnis
Siúd ba chleachtadh dhúinn —
Dá bhfaighinn dul siar air.

Quatrains of Mary Hogan

I

Once I am rid of these meshes —
God send it be soon and forever!
It may not be counted unseemly
My peace in your arms to remember.

When prayer becomes possible to me,
With Mass and receipt of Communion,
Oh, who will declare it indecent
To entreat for myself or for you, love?

But, while we await this conclusion,
Do not grow too deeply enamoured,
For I am committed to loosing
All bonds that could ever be fastened.

II

All ban of priest defying,
Indifferent to all
Suspicion, I am lying
Between you and the wall.

Night's winter weather cannot
Reach here to change my mind —
Warm, secret world and narrow,
Within one bed confined;

What is to come we heed not,
Nor what was done before,
The time is ours, my dearest,
And it will last till dawn.

III

So we must reckon a year
That we the one coverlet share,
Difficult now to be clear
What I wanted, for what came prepared?

Mine was a generous love —
You trampled it under your heel —
With never a question at all
If the flesh that was trodden could feel?

Oh, but the body obeys,
For the sake of a long-given word,
But now that the song in the heart has been stayed
Joy ebbs from our pleasure like tide on the turn.

IV

Infant jealousy feeds at my breast:
I must nurse by day, I must nurse by night;
He's an ugly youngster and teething fast,
And he poisons my veins with his milk-tooth bite.

Don't let the small wretch separate us —
So sound and healthy as was our mating!
Its warrant was skin to skin that clave, and
Its seal a hand granted every favour.

I have no mind to deny affection
Though doubt takes root in deep dejection —
Do not abuse a good draft mare then,
And she, in her own time, will repair all.

V

Oh, what a wonder is pain!
How it gnaws at the cage

Of the ribs! And it will not abate
Or be sated, come night or come day.

Thus it is, pain is made known,
You will never be sole or alone,
But will carry your company close
Like a mother her babe in the womb.

VI

'I do not sleep of nights':
It is not much to say,
But who has yet devised a way to calculate,
Upon the open eye,
How heavy the night's weight.

The night is long!
There were nights once
With you not long —
Which I renounce.

Not hard to follow
The road I went;
No longer possible
If I repent.

We lay for mirth
And we rose with gladness —
Practices such
As I must abandon.

Translated by the author

Mary Hogan, the mistress of the eighteenth-century poet Donncha Rua Mac Conmara, is the archetype of the unhappy female lover in Irish folklore.

Codladh an Ghaiscígh

Ceannín mogallach milis mar sméar —
A mhaicín iasachta, a chuid an tsaoil,
Dé do bheathasa is neadaigh im chroí,
Dé do bheathasa fé fhrathacha an tí,
A réilthín maidine 'tháinig i gcéin.

Is maith folaíocht isteach!
Féach mo bhullán beag d'fhear:
Sáraigh sa doras é nó ceap
I dtubán — Chomh folláin le breac
Gabhaimse orm! Is gach ball fé rath,
An áilleacht mar bharr ar an neart —

Do thugais ón bhfómhar do dhath
Is ón rós crón. Is deas
Gach buí óna chóngas leat.
Féach, a Chonchúir, ár mac,
Ní mar beartaíodh ach mar cheap
Na cumhachta in airde é 'theacht.

Tair go dtím' bachlainn, a chircín eornan,
Tá an lampa ar lasadh is an oíche ag tórmach,
Tá an mada rua ag siúl an bóthar,
Nár sheola aon chat mara ag snapadh é id threosa,
Nuair gur coinneal an teaghlaigh ar choinnleoirín
    óir tú.

Id shuan duit fém' borlach
Is fál umat mo ghean —
Ar do chamachuaird má sea
Fuar agam bheith dhed' bhrath.

Cén chosaint a bhéarfair leat?
Artha? Leabharúin? Nó geas?
'Ná taobhaigh choíche an geal,'
Paidir do chine le ceart.

Ar nós gach máthar seal
Deinim mo mhachnamh thart
Is le linn an mheabhraithe
Siúd spíonóig mhaide id ghlaic!
Taibhrítear dom go pras
An luan láich os do chneas
I leith is gur chugham a bheadh,
Garsúinín Eamhna, Cú na gCleas!

The Hero's Sleep

Blackberry-sweet, the little clustered head!
Small foreign son, my share of this world's treasure,
Nest and be welcome underneath my heart;
Nest and be welcome underneath our rafters;
You've come a long way, little morning star.

It is good so to breed, from without:
See my manling, my little bull-calf —
Head him off from the door, trap him safe in his bath —
On my word, he's as sound as a trout,
In every limb prospering stoutly,
In strength, and in beauty to crown it.

You took your colour from the Autumn
And from the dun rose:
Lovely all yellows! They are your relations —
Look, Conor, here then our son,

162

Not as his advent was planned,
But as Providence put it in hand.

My small barley hen, let me gather you in;
The night's darkness threatens, the lamp has been lit;
The fox is abroad on the roads —
No ill-hap send him snapping to our door,
Where you shine, the household's candle, on a candle-
    stick of gold!

Asleep beneath my breast
My love has walled you in,
But when your kingly steps go forth,
I dog your path in vain.
What charm will keep you safe?
What talisman prevail?
Is not 'No treaty with the white!'
Your proper tribal prayer?

As is a mother's way,
I let my thoughts run on,
And while my mind debates,
You've seized the wooden spoon!
At once my dream is changed,
Your hero's light shines round —
Just such another little boy,
They say, was Ulster's Hound.

Translated by the author

Oíche Nollag

Le coinnle na n-aingeal tá an spéir amuigh breactha,
Tá fiacail an tseaca sa ghaoith ón gcnoc,
Adaigh an tine is téir chun na leapan,
Luífidh Mac Dé ins an tigh seo anocht.

Fágaidh an doras ar leathadh ina coinne,
An mhaighdean a thiocfaidh is a naí ar a hucht,
Deonaigh do shuaimhneas a ligint, a Mhuire,
Luíodh Mac Dé ins an tigh seo anocht.

Bhí soilse ar lasadh i dtigh sin na haíochta,
Cóiriú gan caoile, bia agus deoch,
Do cheannaithe olla, do cheannaithe síoda,
Ach luífidh Mac Dé ins an tigh seo anocht.

Christmas Eve

With candles of angels the sky is now dappled
The frost on the wind from the hills has a bite
Kindle the fire and go to your slumber
Jesus will lie in this household tonight.

Leave all the doors wide open before her
The Virgin who'll come with the child on her breast
Grant that you'll stop here tonight, Holy Mary,
That Jesus tonight in this household may rest.

The lights were all lighting in that little hostel,
There were generous servings of victuals and wine
For merchants of silk, for merchants of woollens
But Jesus will lie in this household tonight.

Translated by Gabriel Fitzmaurice

TOMÁS Mac SÍOMÓIN

Born in Dublin in 1938, Tomás Mac Síomóin is a graduate of UCD and Cornell University, New York where he received his doctorate in plant pathology. He has published four collections of poetry and one translation with Douglas Sealy of Máirtín Ó Direáin's poetry. Currently editor of *Comhar* and a lecturer in Applied Biology at the College of Technology in Kevin St, Dublin, he is working on a cultural history of eighteenth- and nineteenth-century Ireland.

Celan

Stroic crag airgid croí Celan
Glan eascartha amach as cis a chráimh
Is thit a dhaingean síos isteach
I mbóchna bhaoth an bháis.
Ach mhair an briathar a chan sé an oíche úd.
Ag bóithreoireacht feadh na mblianta
Gur sháigh an eochair i mbeo mo chré
A d'oscail athuair an chréacht úd.
Is féach, a Celan, fuil chraorag do chroí
A' sileadh thar chab mo dháin
Is an síol a chuiris fadó riamh
Ag scoilteadh leac an bháis.

Celan

A silver claw tore Celan's heart
Clean out of its cage of bone
And down his ramparts tumbled
Into Death's idiot ocean.
But the word he sang that night lived
On and roamed the roads of time,
Placed a key in living clay
That opened again the wound.
And, Celan, see your heart's red blood
Spurt across this lip of Gaelic verse;
See the seed you planted then
Split the mould of death.

Translated by the author

CAITLÍN MAUDE

Caitlín Maude was born in Connemara, Co Galway in 1941. She studied English, Irish, French and mathematics at UCG, attaining first place in French in her first year there. She worked as a teacher. She was involved in drama in UCG and later with An Taibhdhearc in Galway and the Damer Theatre in Dublin. She wrote, with Michael Hartnett, one play, *An Lasair Choille*. A musician and sean-nós singer, in 1975 Gael Linn published an LP of her poetry and singing called, simply, *Caitlín*. A lifelong Irish language activist, she died on June 6 1982. In 1984, Coiscéim published a book of her poems, *Caitlín Maude — Dánta*.

Aimhréidh

Siúil, a ghrá,
cois trá anocht —
siúil agus cuir uait
na deora —
éirigh agus siúil anocht

    ná feac do ghlúin feasta
    ag uaigh sin an tsléibhe
tá na blátha sin feoite
agus tá mo chnámhasa dreoite ...

    (Labhraim leat anocht
    ó íochtar mara —
    labhraim leat gach oíche
    ó íochtar mara ...)

shiúileas lá cois trá —
shiúileas go híochtar trá —
rinne tonn súgradh le tonn —
ligh an cúr bán mo chosa —

d'árdaíos mo shúil go mall
'gus ansiúd amuigh ar an domhain
in aimhréidh cúir agus toinne
chonaic an t-uaigneas i do shúil
'gus an doilíos i do ghnúis

shiúileas amach ar an domhain
ó ghlúin go com
agus ó chom go guaille
nó gur slogadh mé
sa doilíos 'gus san uaigneas

Entanglement

Walk, my love,
by the strand tonight —
walk, and away
with tears —
arise and walk tonight

    henceforth never bend your knee
    at that mountain grave
those flowers have withered
and my bones decayed ...

    (I speak to you tonight
    from the bottom of the sea —
    I speak to you each night
    from the bottom of the sea ...)

once I walked on the strand —
I walked to the tide's edge —
wave played with wave —

the white foam licked my feet —
I slowly raised my eye
and there far out on the deep
in the tangle of foam and wave
I saw the loneliness in your eye
the sorrow in your face

I walked out on the deep
from knee to waist
and from waist to shoulder
until I was swallowed
in sorrow and loneliness

Translated by Gabriel Fitzmaurice

Amhrán Grá Vietnam

Dúirt siad go raibh muid gan náir
ag ceiliúr ár ngrá
agus an scrios seo inár dtimpeall

an seabhac ag guairdeall san aer
ag feitheamh le boladh an bháis

dúirt siad gurbh iad seo ár muintir féin
gurbh í seo sochraide ár muintire
gur chóir dúinn bheith sollúnta féin
bíodh nach raibh brónach

ach muidne
tá muid 'nós na haimsire
go háirid an ghrian

ní thugann muid mórán aird'
ar imeachtaí na háite seo feasta

lobhann gach rud le teas na gréine
thar an mbás

agus ní muidne a mharaigh iad
ach sibhse

d'fhéadfadh muid fanacht ar pháirc an áir
ach chuir aighthe brónacha na saighdiúirí
ag gáirí sinn
agus thogh muid áit bhog cois abhann

Vietnam Love Song

They said that we were shameless
celebrating our love
with devastation all around us

the hawk hovering in the air
awaiting the stench of death

they said that these were our own
that this was the funeral of our own people
that we should at least be solemn
even if we were not mourning

but we
we are like the weather
      especially the sun
we don't pay much attention
to these happenings any longer

everything decays in the heat of the sun
after death

and it wasn't we who killed them
but you

we could have stayed on the field of slaughter
but the sad faces of the soldiers
made us laugh
and we chose a soft place by the river

Translated by Gabriel Fitzmaurice

Géibheann

Ainmhí mé

ainmhí allta
as na teochreasa
        a bhfuil cliú agus cáil
        ar mo scéimh

chroithfinn crainnte na coille
tráth
le mo gháir

ach anois
luím síos
agus breathnaím trí leathsúil
ar an gcrann aonraic sin thall

tagann na céadta daoine
chuile lá

a dhéanfadh rud ar bith
dom
ach mé a ligean amach

Captivity

I am an animal

a wild animal
from the tropics
    famous
    for my beauty

I would shake the trees of the forest
once
with my cry

but now
I lie down
and observe with one eye
the lone tree yonder

people come in hundreds
every day

who would do anything
for me
but set me free

Translated by Gabriel Fitzmaurice

Impí

A ógánaigh,
ná tar i mo dháil,
ná labhair ...
is binn iad
briathra grá —
is binne aríst
an friotal
nár dúradh ariamh —
níl breith
gan smál —
breith briathar
amhlaidh atá
is ní bheadh ann
ach 'rogha an dá dhíogh'
ó tharla
an scéal mar 'tá ...

ná bris
an ghloine ghlan
'tá eadrainn
  (ní bristear gloine
  gan fuil is pian)
óir tá Neamh
nó Ifreann thall
'gus cén mhaith Neamh
mura mairfidh sé
go bráth? —
ní Ifreann
go hIfreann
iar-Neimhe ...

impím aríst,
ná labhair,
a ógánaigh,
a 'Dhiarmaid',
is beidh muid
suaimhneach —
an tuiscint do-theangmhaithe
eadrainn
gan gair againn
drannadh leis
le saol na saol
is é dár mealladh
de shíor —
ach impím ...
ná labhair ...

Entreaty

Young man,
do not come near me,
do not speak ...
the words of love
are sweet —
but sweeter still
is the word
that was never uttered —
no choice
is without stain —
the choice of words
is much the same
and this would be
to choose between evils
in our present
situation ...

Do not break
the clear glass
between us
  (no glass is broken
  without blood and pain)
for beyond is Heaven
or beyond is Hell
and what good is Heaven
if it is not
for ever? —
the loss of
Heaven
is the worst Hell ...

I again implore you,
do not speak,
young man,
my 'Diarmaid',
and we will be at peace —
untouchable understanding
between us
we will have no cause
to touch it
ever
as it ever
allures us —
but I implore you ...
do not speak ...

Translated by Gabriel Fitzmaurice

PAULA MEEHAN

Born in Dublin in 1955, Paula Meehan studied at Trinity College, Dublin, and at Eastern Washington University. She received Arts Council bursaries in literature in 1987 and 1990. Her poetry collections are *Return and No Blame* (Beaver Row Press 1984), *Reading the Sky* (Beaver Row Press 1985) and *The Man who was Marked by Winter* (Gallery Press 1991). She lives in Dublin.

The Statue of the Virgin at Granard Speaks

It can be bitter here at times like this,
November wind sweeping across the border.
Its seeds of ice would cut you to the quick.
The whole town tucked up safe and dreaming,
even wild things gone to earth, and I
stuck up here in this grotto, without as much as
star or planet to ease my vigil.

The howling won't let up. Trees
cavort in agony as if they would be free
and take off — ghost voyagers
on the wind that carries intimations
of garrison towns, walled cities, ghetto lanes
where men hunt each other and invoke
the various names of God as blessing
on their death tactics, their night manoeuvres.
Closer to home the wind sails over
dying lakes. I hear fish drowning.
I taste the stagnant water mingled
with turf smoke from outlying farms.

They call me Mary — Blessed, Holy, Virgin.
They fit me to a myth of a man crucified:
the scourging and the falling, and the falling again,
the thorny crown, the hammer blow of iron
into wrist and ankle, the sacred bleeding heart.

They name me Mother of all this grief
though mated to no mortal man.
They kneel before me and their prayers
fly up like sparks from a bonfire
that blaze a moment, then wink out.

It can be lovely here at times. Springtime,
early summer. Girls in Communion frocks
pale rivals to the riot in the hedgerows
of cow parsley and haw blossom, the perfume
from every rushy acre that's left for hay
when the light swings longer with the sun's push north.

Or the grace of a midsummer wedding
when the earth herself calls out for coupling
and I would break loose of my stony robes,
pure blue, pure white, as if they had robbed
a child's sky for their colour. My being
cries out to be incarnate, incarnate,
maculate and tousled in a honeyed bed.

Even an autumn burial can work its own pageantry.
The hedges heavy with the burden of fruiting
crab, sloe, berry, hip; clouds scud east
pear scented, windfalls secret in long
orchard grasses, and some old soul is lowered
to his kin. Death is just another harvest
scripted to the season's play.

But on this All Souls' Night there is
no respite from the keening of the wind.
I would not be amazed if every corpse came risen
from the graveyard to join in exaltation with the gale,
a cacophony of bone imploring sky for judgement
and release from being the conscience of the town.

On a night like this I remember the child
who came with fifteen summers to her name,
and she lay down alone at my feet
without midwife or doctor or friend to hold her hand
and she pushed her secret out into the night,
far from the town tucked up in little scandals,
bargains struck, words broken, prayers, promises,
and though she cried out to me in extremis
I did not move,
I didn't lift a finger to help her,
I didn't intercede with heaven,
nor whisper the charmed word in God's ear.

On a night like this I number the days to the solstice
and the turn back to the light.
                                        O sun,
centre of our foolish dance,
burning heart of stone,
molten mother of us all,
hear me and have pity.

TOM MORGAN

Born in Ligoniel, Belfast in 1943, Tom Morgan was Head of English in St Augustine's High School, Belfast. To date *The Rat-Diviner, Nan of the Falls Rd, Curfew* (both from Beaver Row Press) and *In Queen Mary's Gardens* (Salmon) have been published. He has just completed a new book on Ligoniel and Ballintrillick, Co Sligo, with a BBC Northern Ireland broadcast due in the near future.

Easter in the West

There is hay on his jumper from feeding cattle;
a hairy old crombie flaps in the wind.
His walk is slow and his talk is steady, explaining
whitethorn and blackthorn, rowan and sally.

He thumbs towards the background and eyes North.
A place beyond his reckoning, he's a veteran of
cattle, foxes and sheep, the wind's direction,
or the colour of scree on the edge of the mountain.

How are things up there, he asks politely; but,
being tired to reply, I avoid its complexity,
ask about people, the mart or the harvest,
who's alive or dead, gone mad or happy.

When his feet change from turf at the edge of the bog,
he soon finds his place in the spirit-grocers.
An empty crate with his back to the fridge with
a view of the door or the street and the bridge.

When I ask about weather, he eyes me as a stranger,
his face stares the floor as he ponders on his answer:
'If the new moon's on its back, it's a sign of rain;
but how could a downpour be caught in a saucer?'

Haven

Between the years of four and seven,
the pithead and the meadow were my haven.

The parish hall was at my feet
the church above my head
and mornings after concerts
I fled the warmth of bed.

78's were dumped there
a feast for the eyes to see,
and how I loved smashing
McCormick and Gallicurci.

Behind the parish priest's house,
above the old brickyard,
I sniffed crushed nettles
and learned to fall hard.

On little bits of timber,
or corrugated tin,
I raised the dust off cinders
wore burn marks on my skin.

Between the years of four and seven,
the pithead and the meadow were my haven.

The Aspidistra

For Jane and Nellie

In an alcove on the landing
stood a plant without a flower;
a polished aspidistra
in a purple Chinese jar.

On wet April evenings
or early in July, we'd jump
the first steep flight of stairs
and play there near the sky.

It was our favourite hideout
far from school and church and bars,
or the raspy Belfast voices
raised in anger down the stairs.

And if the priest or sergeant
paid their weekly social call,
two cousins and their sisters
fled the mosaic marbled hall.

One evening in October not
far from All Souls' Night,
granda told us stories which
made hair itch with fright.

One was of the landing where
a sickened man had died,
found hanging in the morning
by aunts who screeched and lied.

His eyes had popped their sockets,
his face was darkly pale, and when
they cut his dead weight down
they hammered in the nails.

But very shortly after
a strange event occurred,
the spreading aspidistra
dropped dying near the birds.

It lay like that for seasons
its flesh a sickly grey, but on
the following All Souls' Night
its leaves put on display.

It grew and grew much stronger
its sheen the deepest green,
and for sixty long years after
mocked the hanging beam.

When his story ended,
with faces scared and red,
we eyed one another and
quietly stole to bed.

No standing at the doorway
or talking to the jar,
or playing in a garden of
Chinese petalled flowers,

but straight to bed to shiver
in a darkness near complete,
but for a shaft of gaslight
from the landing near our feet.

GERRY MURPHY

Gerry Murphy was born in Cork. His published works are *A Small Fat Boy Walking Backwards* (Commons Press 1985/Three Spires Press 1992), a pamphlet *A Cartoon History of the Spanish Civil War* (Three Spires Press 1991) and his second collection just issued from Dedalus, *Rio De La Plata And All That*.

Happy Days with the Sendero Luminoso
(for Pat Cotter)

Not wanting to alienate the villagers
we approached the village elder
and asked, *very* politely
if we could spend a few days
recuperating in his village
after our latest battle
with the fascist government thugs.
He answered, that however much
he supported our heroic struggle, and there was
                                        nobody
who supported it more than he, nevertheless
he had to consider the welfare of the villagers
and could not be seen to take sides,
since the army would inevitably learn of our stay,
come and shoot him and destroy his village.
We could only interpret this as a lack of
                                 revolutionary
fervour amongst the peasantry and further evidence
of a growing apathy towards the struggle.

So we shot him and destroyed his village.

PAUL MURRAY

Paul Murray was born in Newcastle, Co Down in 1947, educated at St Malachy's College, Belfast and entered the Dominican Order in 1966. His books include *Ritual Poems* (New Writers' Press 1971), *Rites and Meditations* (Dolmen 1982) and *The Absent Fountain* (Dedalus Press 1992).

Meditation IX

Not the naked sudden thought
of this or that lovely girl,
the sudden impulse, the desire to take
into my arms for a brief moment
the sensual, midnight spouse.
Not that which in the mind is natural
to imagine, natural to affirm: the most
ordinary, most obvious answer
to a grown man's fullest need.
Not that calmness therefore, not even
with the trembling of desire appeased,
that dark spontaneous joining together
in one flesh, of man and woman,
that brief perfect equilibrium.
And yet, at times, I know that in my
being you have touched me, Lord:
the stark passion of desire
is calmed, and calm is passionate.

Widow

Certainly as children we never thought
of them as lovers.
She moved within the compass

of his needs and turned to him
so naturally.
There was always time

to make his quiet unobtrusive
fate her own,
gradually to be woven

into the pattern of his changing moods
and even to accommodate unchanging
fears like waking up

alone in hospital, — she'd stay there
half the night just watching him.
Without direction now,

awkward among her married
sons and daughters, she comes and goes
like Santa Claus.

ÁINE Ní GHLINN

Born in 1955 in Co Tipperary, Áine Ní Ghlinn works as a journalist with RTE and Raidio na Gaeltachta. She has had two collections of poetry published by Coiscéim: *An Chéim Bhriste* (1984) and *Gairdín Pharthais* (1988). She is at present working on a third collection.

An Chéim Bhriste

Cloisim thú agus tú ag teacht aníos an staighre.
Siúlann tú ar an gcéim bhriste. Seachnaíonn gach
éinne í ach siúlann tusa i gcónaí uirthi.

D'fhiafraigh tú díom céard é m'ainm. Bhíomar le
chéile is dúirt tú go raibh súile gorma agam.

Má fheiceann tú solas na gréine ag deireadh an lae is
má mhúsclaíonn sé thú chun filíocht a scríobh ...
    Sin é m'ainm.

Má thagann tú ar cuairt chugam is má bhíonn 'fhios
agam gur tusa atá ann toisc go gcloisim do choiscéim
    ar an staighre ...
    Sin é m'ainm.

Dúirt tú gur thuig tú is go raibh mo shúile gorm.
Shiúil tú arís uirthi is tú ag imeacht ar maidin.

Tagann tú isteach sa seomra is feicim ó do shúile go
raibh tú léi. Ní labhrann tú ná ní fhéachann tú ar mo
shúile. Tá a cumhracht ag sileadh uait.

Tá an chumhracht caol ard dea-dhéanta is tá a gruaig
fada agus casta. Cloisim thú ag insint di go bhfuil a
súile gorm is go bhfuil tú i ngrá léi.

Osclaím an doras agus siúlann tú amach.
D'fhéadfá é a mhíniú dhom a dheir tú. Dúnaim
   an doras.

Ní shiúlann tú uirthi. Seachnaíonn tú an chéim
bhriste. Ní shiúlann éinne ar an gcéim bhriste.
Déantar í a sheachaint i gcónaí.

The Broken Step

I hear you when you climb the stairs. You walk
on the broken step. Everyone else avoids it, but
you walk on it always.

You asked me what my name was. We were together
and you said my eyes were blue.

If you see sunlight at nightfall and if
it awakens a poem in you ...
   That's my name.

If you visit me and I know it's you
because I hear your footstep on the stair ...
   That's my name.

You said you understood and that my eyes were blue.
You walked again on it when you left this morning.

You come into the room and I see from your eyes that
you were with her. You do not speak nor do you look
into my eyes. Her fragrance flows from you.

The fragrance is slender, tall, well-formed, and her
hair is long and curling. I hear you tell her that her
eyes are blue and that you love her.

I open the door and you walk out.
You can explain you tell me. I close
   the door.

You do not walk on it. You avoid the broken step.
No-one walks on the broken step. They avoid it
always.

Translated by Gabriel Fitzmaurice

Mórtas Cine

Caithfear a admháil
gur doirteadh fuil ár sinsear
gur bádh iad
ina dtonntracha fola féin
gur lig siad scread
is iad ag dul go tóin
gur dhein an scread macalla
a dhein macalla
a dhein macalla
a dhéanann fós macalla
inár gcuisleacha inniu.

Is cé go bhfuil an scread
dár stróiceadh óna chéile
go gcoinnímid beo í
ar eagla go gcreidfí
nárbh fhiú
saothar ár sinsear.

Racial Pride

It must be admitted
that our ancestors' blood was shed
that they were drowned
in the waves of their own blood
that they cried out
as they were sinking
that their cry echoed
echoed
echoed
and echoes still
in our veins.

And though that cry
is tearing us apart
we keep it alive
lest anyone believe
that our ancestors' labour
was not worthwhile.

Translated by Gabriel Fitzmaurice

PAT O'BRIEN

Born in Claremorris, Co Mayo in 1951, Pat O'Brien is a priest of Tuam diocese working in Skehana, East Galway. His publications are *Book of Genesis* (1988), editor of *Erect Me a Monument of Broken Wings: Writings by and on Padraig Fallon* (1992) and *Tulips in the Prison Yard; Selected Poems of Daniel Berrigan, Selected and Introduced by Pat O'Brien* (1992).

Ever After

I will tell you how it ends.
I am the man who was the child
who spoke aloud the emperor's nakedness.
I have lived to regret the words. Friends
became distant, disappeared. My name was filed
away for future reference. A great sadness

began in our land. A twenty year terror.
The laughter of the crowd at my remark
quickly turned to tears — martial law
applied with ferocity. It is said the emperor
took personal responsibility for the dark
age. Executions and reprisals he oversaw,

with eyes turned cruel. The day I came of age
his soldiers brought an invitation to the palace.
They threw me into prison, stripped my clothes.
Each night he visits me in my cold cage.
His splendid uniforms are bemedalled. What solace
is mine when, nightly, the doors close.

On That Day

On that day of freedom and equality
avoid the streets of the city,
loud with celebrations.

Go, rather, to the sea's shore,
as you did on all the days before,
and hear its quiet cautions.

JULIE O'CALLAGHAN

Born in Chicago in 1954, Julie O'Callaghan has lived in Ireland for twenty years. Her publications include *Edible Anecdotes* (Dolmen 1983) and *What's What* (Bloodaxe 1991), a Poetry Book Society Choice.

---

from *Edible Anecdotes*

14

look at it this way, cookie
ya wanna make it big
or ya wanna spend the rest a yer life
playing bit parts in dog food commercials?
sweetheart, I know it ain't gonna be easy
but no one is gonna hire a two-ton-tessy
for their swanky prime-time serial
with designer wardrobe the way it costs
ya gotta cut out the Sara Lee Cheesecake
and the Pepperidge Farm Chocolate Chips
that's all there is to it
listen, honey, you got the talent
and nobody likes the fuller figure better'n me
but the Liz Taylor physique just ain't in
sure, I'll help ya, casting's in three weeks
so you'll eat celery and drink sugar-free cola
till ya fit into a size 10 cocktail dress
you'll look a million dollars
now go empty out your kitchen
and no cheatin cuz I'll be over
to check up on ya

26

'No meat onry lice,
walk ar day an get no meat.
Keep walk for thlee mon in jungr,
no stop.
At night, a file to be walm
sometime fish — onry thlee o fou time.
Een litr chiren keep walk, no shoe
feets at begin ouch, ouch, ouch
stand on locks
then get tough, no yerp.
Evly night sreep on mud, no house.
Aftel sreep olang maybe,
sometime no food.
Pol Pot bad man.
Cambodia boo-how.
Now chirens is safe.
I go to the chicken
I mean, kitchen
and cook pea pod, lice, pok,
mushloom, bean splout, watel chestnut
and arways give some to peopres
who rook hungly,
say, "eat, eat"'

CLAIRR O'CONNOR

Born in Limerick in 1951, Clairr O'Connor now lives in Maynooth, Co Kildare. She was educated at St Mary's Convent, Limerick, UCC and St Patrick's College, Maynooth. She has published a collection of poetry, *When You Need Them* (Salmon 1989) and a novel, *Belonging* (Attic Press 1991) and was nominated for the *Irish Times*/Aer Lingus Award. She has been published in Irish, English and American journals and collections and has also written for the stage and radio. She is currently working on her second novel.

Listening to Cindy

'Where do they put all the breasts
they cut off anyhow?'
'Best not think on it, honey,'
soothes Don.
'I wanna think on it.
It's part of me I no longer have.
I've been having nightmares —
breasts floating above the city
or moving along the sidewalk
offering nipples to passersby.
Everywhere I look —
sucklings gumming furiously.
You know, back in the sixties
when everyone was having free
range kids, I was embarrassed —
but being a coward I settled
into breast is best too.
Seemed like all the earth's
kids were sucking on me.
My rivers kept on flowing.
I guess I looked the part

in my paisley dress.
Right now I wanna be left
in these white walls, honey.
I just don't wanna
play-act no more.'

ULICK O'CONNOR

Born in Dublin in 1928, Ulick O'Connor studied at UCD where he took a degree in law. Biographer, poet and playwright, his poetry collections are *Sputnik and Other Poems* (Devin-Adair Company 1967), *Life Styles* (Dolmen/Hamish Hamilton 1973), *All Things Counter* (Dedalus 1986) and *One is Animate* (Beaver Row Press 1990). His verse plays in the Noh form were first produced by the Abbey Theatre in 1977 and later at the Dublin Theatre Festival in 1979. They received an off-Broadway production in 1981. His play *Execution* broke attendance records at the Peacock Theatre in Autumn 1985. He was a member of the Board of Directors of the Abbey Theatre 1981-1985.

Easter Week 1986

I

It slowly oozed out
Till seventy years now
It might not have been.
No Government to bow
Or soldier's trumpet call
In memory of your deed
At Kilmainham wall.
Was it just a dream
Scorned in our waking hours,
That proved in the cold light
Beyond our powers.
Have we paid the price
For your sacrifice?

II

Awake now for seventy years
Long lines of the hopeless file.
Yes: they are kept alive
In approved imperial style.

III

Though we have conquered in our own way,
Using another tongue to spell
That our empire is of the word
And can dominate as well
As Roman wall or Norman tower,
We are still living in pawn.
Divided, exhausted, confused spectators
Of an uneasy dawn,
While police fire above the head
Of crowds, for imagined slights,
Their backs turned on that sacrificial shed.
How long before they lower their sights?

Ernesto Lynch-Guevara

(Assassinated Bolivia, November 1968)

The trouble with revolutions
Is that they usually end up
With the same solutions
As the crowd they've sent up,
But you, when the job was done
And spoils for the taking,
Went off to the next one
Without waiting.
Like a poet, who won't hear
An old poem played back,
You got yourself in the clear,
Cut a new track.

It never made the charts
But it's going to be around
When the next one starts
And they need a new sound.

Homage to Sean MacBride (Died 16th July 1988)
(Winner of Nobel Prize for Peace and Lenin Peace Prize)

Always I remember you in that house
Standing at the door to welcome us,
The touch of the seigneur in your stance,
But the warmth of the chieftain in your glance.
Then, noticing as the night wore on
    How her presence filled the room
    Like the scent of a faint perfume
That lingers after the beloved has gone.

In your talk legends were begotten —
'W.B. taught me English; Ezra, Latin'.
And the mind recalled what the poet had said —
'That straight back and arrogant head'.
In this forge she shaped what she held dear
    To free Ireland and release her sex
    From man-made laws, this was her text.
Constance, Hannah, Charlotte all worked here.

You had the comprehension without which
There is no making sense of this crazy pitch,
How someone bred from high intent and creed
May tip the scales, unleash a fearful deed.
Yet had not that cast of mind prevailed,

Slouched like a dolt beside the fire
Savouring his anger like desire,
Would have let the pot simmer till it boiled.

In that book-lined room I watched many a night
You finger out a clause, begin the fight
To save some man; with dawn the firelight danced
On those high cheekbones, and the mind had chanced
On that fantastic knight; could one man find
 So much to joust against and win?
 Armoured with argument you went in,
Your lance the lightning flourish of the mind.

Now at your funeral a Cardinal talks,
Yeats' verses clamour through the vaults,
Lenin too, is named. So much has changed
Through you. At your grave the Army ranged
To present arms. The same, which from your cell
 Took Rory to the firing squad.
 But that, too, has been turned to good,
More accomplished by a guiding will.

Through the streets the funeral takes its way,
An old woman grasps me by the hand to say —
'You could listen to her all night'. That face
Again intrudes upon our space,
You and she in that great tale revealed,
 Which he thought alone worthy of theme,
 The people's book which holds the dream
When all that's left of Tara is a field.

Making Out

This guy was coming against the traffic in a way that was
   outlandish
Hunched in a wheelchair, his hands whirling like a dervish,
Brushing one car like a ballerina balancing against her
   danseur,
Then with maniacal dexterity missing the next one by a
   hair.

Between the gleaming ranks I glimpsed your agonised
   fierce gaze,
To go against the stream is how you shape your praise
Of life: as in your iron cage, which you steer with such
   panache,
You destabilise commuters with this mad frenetic dash.

With their misbegotten rock, the gods screwed the
   unfortunate Sisyphus,
But you with your own rock, put on a show that shames
   the best of us,
You've asked from life no meaning — which makes the
   gods redundant
By seeking within yourself a god, in your skirmish on the
   pavement.

HUGH O'DONNELL

Born in Dublin in 1951, Hugh O'Donnell studied Arts and Theology. He was ordained a priest in 1977. His collection of poetry, *Roman Pines at Berkeley*, was published by Salmon Publishing in 1990.

My Niece Nearly Five

Cramped conditions favour her at four;
she twirls on a sixpence into dance
routines unrehearsed, broadcasts
original compositions through 15 yards
of green hosepipe for silent millions;

highly amused at her lightfoot sense
of fun, she delivers speeches to her
great grandchildren perched on the fence,
berating infants and mothers alike;

if you can be trusted, she will impart
one hundred thousand secrets only
she knows, giving everything away;
in the night sky she is the star beguiling
your exhausted world with fantasy;

the logic of your departure is beyond her,
but having squeezed the life out of you,
she whispers goodbye inside your jacket
where the lining smells of you.

MARY O'DONNELL

Poet, short-story writer, novelist and critic, Mary O'Donnell's novel *The Light-Makers* was published last year. She is currently working on a novel and her new poetry collection will be published next Autumn. She is the presenter of *Along the Backwater*, a poetry request programme on RTE Radio 1.

Antarctica

I do not know what other women know.
I covet their children; wardrobes
stocked with blue or pink, froth-lace
bootees for the animal-child
that bleeds them.

Their calmness settles like the
ebb-tide on island shores —
nursing pearl-conch, secret fronds
of wisdom, certitude.
Their bellies taunt.

I do not know what other women know.
Breasts await the animal-child.
I want — maddened by
lunar crumblings, the false prophecy
of tingling breasts, turgid abdomen.

Antarctica: The storm petrel hovers;
waters petrified by spittled winds:
Little fish will not swim here.
Folds of bed-sheet take my face.
Blood seeps, again.

'But you are free', they cry,
'You have no child!' — bitterness
from women grafted like young willows,
forced before time. In Antarctica,
who will share this freedom?

Stalking

Again, let me say it:
I don't need men who stalk
with the skill of centuries

on hand and tongue, smoke
and rancid flesh making their
blood dance; or men who spy

from a distance, conjure
beauty or love, like warlocks.
I don't need trinkets for

what I am, or disbelief at
my vision, the silence beyond
all journeys. I don't need

illusion, the spear of
your strength, my frailty —
it venoms a soul.

You would encroach on my peace,
to snare it. Your eyes are
greedy, gunged with a briar

of maleness that is not male:
They linger when I laugh —
like a hand on my thigh when

there's no need. Keep
that antique mating-dance,
that honey-flint in your voice

as you bandy love and truth
like trial spearheads.
My sun has risen, fans

a trellis above the trees,
ambers the spruced silence,
makes water dance.

My heart is brim full:
Don't tread too close:
Love my freedom.

Cycling with Martin

This harvest, we whirr across terrain
    once dreamt of, cautious immigrants
        in the land of forgotten love.

Miles breeze past our heads,
    unfasten a week's tidy thoughts
        as we eye the possibilities

in tumbling thickets,
    or sample blackberries,
       find more than sweetness,

a reckless tang bruising the lips.
    I sample your body on such trips,
       draw urgent images from leaves,

long, pushing mushrooms, flaming rosehip,
    idle on the hours we've spent,
       the heat of your buttocks

as you break within me.
    Windflown now, the bikes
       sheer down the last stretch.

This bawdy autumn, I quicken,
    feel vintage warmth in the sun,
       unsprung from myself as the year drowses.

Hungry for peaches and plums,
    flesh lustily cloven,
       I repeat my cyclist's mantra,

brute labials like *love, my love ...*

BERNARD O'DONOGHUE

Bernard O'Donoghue was born in Cullen, Co Cork in 1945. Since 1965 he has lived in Oxford where he teaches English at Magdalen College. He has published books on medieval English literature as well as four volumes of poetry including *Poaching Rights* (Dublin, Gallery 1987) and *The Weakness* (London, Chatto 1991). *The Weakness* was shortlisted for the Whitbread and Forward Prizes.

Finn the Bonesetter

Proverbial wisdom kept us off the streets
And that's a fact. The art of talk is dead.
When we had shaken all our heads enough
At people's knowing in the days of old
(When a cow died they thanked Almighty God
It wasn't one of them), we'd contemplate
Our local marvel-workers. On the flat
Of his back for three years and more, surgeons
Could do nothing: Finn had him walking
The four miles to Mass inside an hour.

Incurably rheumatical myself,
I made him out at home above Rockchapel
Where the swallows purred approving in the eaves.
Bent at a crystal mirror, he was bathing
A red eye. 'I'm praying I won't go blind
From it. Do you know anything about eyes?'
Beyond having heard it said that his descried
The future, I didn't. He rolled his sleeves
Back to his shoulder like an accredited
Inseminator and got down to it.
I'm much relieved and think there's something in it.

Bulmer

How do you know but every bird
That beats the gladsome air
Is an immense world of delight,
Closed by your senses five?

Into Tesco's with me, eight a.m.,
And, cider bottle under my oxter,
Out with a light step, fearing no one.

Sitting on the bridge, I watch them
Haring by, buses, briefcases,
God knows what. You'd be sorry

For the poor misfortunes, with their work
And their temper, but what can you do?
They'd only think they knew better.

One day I saw a woodpecker
Above in the tree: as clear
As I see you now, and as green

As the one on the bottle. I called
In a whisper to this fellow going by,
But he dodged around me, and nearly

Hit the wall. 'You'd only drink it',
He said. Leave him at it. Green
As deep as the kingfisher's blue.

Once I sat for hours, talking
To a little foxy girl, a student
In a duffle coat. There was nothing

She didn't know about birds.
Spring again now, and the sun
Is warm enough to dry the green

Of winter off the bark. I thought
I'd head for London to see
What they make of things down there.

A Noted Judge of Horses

The ache in his right arm worsening
Morning by morning asks for caution.
He knows its boding, cannot be wrong
About this. Yet he is more concerned
For the planks in the float that need
Woodworm treatment before drawing in
The hay, and whether the coarse meadow
Must be limed before it will crop again.

Still in the pallid dawn he dresses
In the clothes she laid out last night,
Washes in cold water and sets off,
Standing in the trailer with his eyes set
On the Shrove Fair. As long as his arm
Can lift a stick to lay in judgement
Down the shuddering line of a horse's back,
He'll take his chance, ignoring his dream
That before September's fair he'll be mumbling
From a hospital bed, pleading with nurses
To loose the pony tied by the western gate.

Munster Final

in memory of Tom Creedon, died 28 August 1983

The jarveys to the west side of the town
Are robbers to a man, and if you tried
To drive through The Gap, they'd nearly strike you
With their whips. So we parked facing for home
And joined the long troop down the meadowsweet
And woodbine-scented road into the town.
By blue Killarney's lakes and glens to see
The white posts on the green! To be deafened
By the muzzy megaphone of Jimmy Shand
And the testy bray to keep the gangways clear.

As for Tom Creedon, I can see him still,
His back arching casually to field and clear.
'Glory Macroom! Good boy, Tom Creedon!'
 We'd be back next year to try our luck in Cork.

We will be back next year, roaring ourselves
Hoarse, praying for better luck. After first Mass
We'll get there early; that's our only hope.
Keep clear of the carparks so we're not hemmed in,
And we'll be home, God willing, for the cows.

A Nun Takes the Veil

That morning early I ran through briars
To catch the calves that were bound for market.
I stopped the once, to watch the sun
Rising over Doolin across the water.

The calves were tethered outside the house
While I had my breakfast: the last one at home
For forty years. I had what I wanted (they said
I could), so we'd loaf bread and Marie biscuits.

We strung the calves behind the boat,
Me keeping clear to protect my style:
Confirmation suit and my patent sandals.
But I trailed my fingers in the cool green water,

Watching the puffins driving homeward
To their nests on Aran. On the Galway mainland
I tiptoed clear of the cow-dunged slipway
And watched my brothers heaving the calves

As they lost their footing. We went in a trap,
Myself and my mother, and I said goodbye
To my father then. The last I saw of him
Was a hat and jacket and a salley stick,

Driving cattle to Ballyvaughan.
He died (they told me) in the county home,
Asking to see me. But that was later:
As we trotted on through the morning mist,

I saw a car for the first time ever,
Hardly seeing it before it vanished.
I couldn't believe it, and I stood up looking
To where I could hear its noise departing

But it was only a glimpse. That night in the convent
The sisters spoilt me, but I couldn't forget
The morning's vision, and I fell asleep
With the engine humming through the open
    window.

The Fool in the Graveyard

When we die, we help each other out
Better than usual.

This was his big day, and he was glad
His Dad was dead, because everyone,
However important or usually
Unfriendly, came up to him and
Solemnly shook his new leather glove
And said 'I'm sorry for your trouble'.
No trouble at all. All these people
Who normally made fun of him
And said, 'What's your name, Dan?'
And laughed when he said 'Dan' (wasn't
That right and polite?), were nice as pie
Today. He'd missed him going to bed
But they'd given him a pound and
An apple and told him a joke.

That made him laugh a bit.
Coming down the aisle, he'd been
At the front with the coffin on
His shoulder, and everyone
Without exception looked straight
At him, some of them nodding gravely
Or mouthing 'How's Dan', and even
Crying, some of them. He'd tried
To smile and nod back, anxious
To encourage kindness. Maybe
They'd always be nice now, remembering
How he'd carried the coffin. Outside
It was very cold, but he had on
The Crombie coat his Dad had bought.

The earth was always yellower
Here than anywhere else, heaped
Next to the grave with its very
Straight sides. How did they dig
The sides so straight? The priest
Led the prayers, and he knew most
Of the answers. Things were looking up.
Today he was like the main actor
In the village play, or the footballer
Who took the frees, or the priest
On the altar. Every eye
Fixed on him! It was like being loved,
And he'd always wondered what that was like.
It wasn't embarrassing at all.

CIARAN O'DRISCOLL

Born in Callan, Co Kilkenny in 1943, Ciaran O'Driscoll now lives in Limerick where he teaches in the School of Art and Design. He has had two collections of poetry published, *Gog and Magog* (Salmon 1987), *The Poet and his Shadow* (Dedalus 1990) and a third, *Listening to Different Drummers*, is due from Dedalus in 1993.

Sunsets and Hernias

They don't have hernias about boiling
lobsters alive: they haven't got the lobsters.
They don't have hernias about the colours
of sunsets — cinnamons, wines and lemons —
because they can't put names on what they see,
and anyway, they haven't got the time
to look, too busy mopping hotel floors,
washing stacks of dishes, looting dustbins.

They don't drown *angst* in hundred-year-old brandies,
and they can't drown their anger in flat beer.
Since sickness means the loss of pay, they save
their hernias as long as they are able,
and can't afford to spend them on the thoughts
of lobsters boiled alive or colours they can't name.

Man with Macaw

This man with a multicoloured bird on his shoulder
often got on the underground at Burnt Oak.
The multicoloured bird shed feathers
that schoolchildren grabbed but mostly
sat mute and trusting on the man's shoulder,
just a little apprehensive, you'd
know that from watching the not-quite-still claws.
Not so much as a squawk from this
serene and multicoloured bird
on the shoulder of a serene-looking
man who wore shabby clothes. They seemed
to lend serenity to one another.
Often he smiled back at smiles,
talked in a matter-of-fact way about
moulting and birdseed, and civilly answered questions.
Always for me his arrival in the carriage
was like the first time I ever saw him,
unobtrusive but slightly wonderful —
Man with Macaw, serene
man and multicoloured bird, children
watching for the fall of a dazzling feather.
Often, because the tube went no further,
we got off at Colindale and waited
for the next one to take us to Burnt Oak:
so ordinary it seemed then, a man
standing on the platform with a macaw on his shoulder,
that stern faces softened and dry tongues
found a couple of friendly words.

Little Old Ladies

Adept at the furtive knee in the groin
and the elbow in the solar plexus,
little old ladies jump the bus queue
waving their out-of-date passes.

On the 16.40 to Raheen,
foraging gangs of three or four
little old ladies surround the conductor
and tell him to stick his peak-hour fare.

Little old ladies conspire to bring
the economy crashing down
by blocking supermarket checkouts
and driving weekend shoppers insane

with an endless supply of pennies counted
out of their moth-eaten purses.
Little old ladies spend their pensions
on knuckledusters and karate courses.

Little old ladies read poems, my foot!
The little old ladies I have seen
on the 16.40 to Raheen
were leafing through manuals of guerilla warfare

and would spit on the *Penguin Book of Contemporary Verse*.
I have seen grown men break down and cry
on the 16.40 to Raheen
when fixed by a little old lady's eye.

DENNIS O'DRISCOLL

Dennis O'Driscoll was born in 1954 in Thurles, Co Tipperary. A widely-published critic of poetry and a former editor of *Poetry Ireland Review*, he is author of three collections of poetry: *Kist* (Dolmen Press 1982), *Hidden Extras* (Anvil /Dedalus 1987) and *Long Story Short* (Anvil/Dedalus 1993).

Someone

someone is dressing up for death today, a change of skirt
                                   or tie
eating a final feast of buttered sliced pan, tea
scarcely having noticed the erection that was his last
shaving his face to marble for the icy laying-out
spraying with deodorant her coarse armpit grass
someone today is leaving home on business
saluting, terminally, the neighbours who will join in the
                                   cortège
someone is trimming his nails for the last time, a precious
                                  moment
someone's thighs will not be streaked with elastic in the
                                  future
someone is putting out milkbottles for a day that will not
                                  come
someone's fresh breath is about to be taken clean away
someone is writing a cheque that will be marked 'drawer
                                deceased'
someone is circling posthumous dates on a calendar
someone is listening to an irrelevant weather forecast
someone is making rash promises to friends
someone's coffin is being sanded, laminated, shined
who feels this morning quite as well as ever

someone if asked would find nothing remarkable in
today's date
perfume and goodbyes her final will and testament
someone today is seeing the world for the last time
as innocently as he had seen it first

Ars Editoria

each body of work is tested by the surgeon
for the regularity of its beat:
he scans it thoroughly for jarring rhythms, stress
rejects superfluous appendices and checks the x-ray's
    proofs

his failures are remaindered, their circulation stopped

Flat Life

I
We listen to noises they must make to live:
window-box of television, a perennial bloom,
world now gazes through;
stylus injecting records against silence;
telephone arguments; top-40 shows . . .

Tonight, even thunder adds percussive sounds,
forked tongues of lightning poison sky.
When, eventually, you sleep
I strain for murmurs from your heart,
the soothing metre of your breath.

But, draining beer tins, tapping denim legs,
tenants still watch detectives shoot
behind bulletproof T.V. glass,
or ears are stereo receivers for rock beat,
dead language of disc-jockeys kills their time.

II
Mornings here are quiet.
Water from spring showers
gargles in dry soil, sprinkles grass.
A grey fur of dust grows over our possessions.
Early swallows skim across an ocean-blue sky,

the few white clouds like foam;
their circling a ripple on its still water.
Silence and water are my natural elements
before speakers deface quiet, scattering its dust.
Your body is still sunk under blankets,

covers rising and falling like a sea
that laps now to your breathing, a great lungfish;
as a shaft of sun filters through the window
blowing the room, like glass, into a globe,
a sudden bubble of frail light.

'O My America!'

The few US-published kids' books
in the Thurles library
felt and smelt as differently
from the usual Puffins and Antelopes
as Tipperary does from Illinois.
We were growing apart

before growing together,
not knowing yet
what in the world we would be
when we grew up:
me straggling from school
with a Milroy macaroon bar,
your small lips smothered
by Hershey's Kisses.
It is Fall — not Autumn —
in this children's book.
Trees bulge in a wind
that dusts the grass off,
polishing its surface.
A little dog, ears flying,
leaps up to unwinding leaves
as if sniffing the offal
of a dying year.
The boys are given crew cuts
in 'full-color illustrations';
they wear plaid lumber jackets
and scream names into the storm
that sound like Chuck and Chester.
No-one answers to your name
among the Cathy Annes and Debbies,
until a freckled girl is seen
waving from a slatted house,
her hair in braids,
her smooth face notched with dimples:
she could be the one
whose photograph I cherish
in my wallet now.

Normally Speaking

To assume everything has meaning.
To return at evening
feeling you have earned a rest
and put your feet up
before a glowing TV set and fire.
To have your favourite shows.
To be married to a local
whom your parents absolutely adore.
To be satisfied with what you have,
the neighbours, the current hemline,
the dual immersion, the government doing its best.
To keep to an average size
and buy clothes off the rack.
To bear the kind of face
that can be made-up to prettiness.
To head contentedly for work
knowing how bored you'd be at home.
To book holidays to where bodies blend,
tanned like sandgrains.
To be given to little excesses,
Christmas hangovers, spike high heels,
chocolate éclair binges, lightened hair.
To postpone children until the house extension
can be afforded and the car paid off.
To see the world through double glazing
and find nothing wrong.
To expect to go on living like this
and to look straight forward. No regrets.
To get up each day neither in wonder nor in fear,
meeting people on the bus you recognise
and who accept you, without question, for what you are.

Time-Sharing

In our time together
we are travelling in the heated car,
a violin concerto playing on the radio,
hills streaming with winter cold,
year-end fields worn down to seams,
a blazing quiff of distant dogwood,
burned meringue of snow on mountain tops.

We blurt past farms and cottages:
those whose era we share
are staring from net curtains
at a morning chill for milking
or for setting off to factories in the town,
their segments of road deserted.
It is like a childhood journey

of sleep and open-eyed surprise,
of hermetically sealed life
in the eternal present
before the final destination is reached.
We hold hands on the gear stick
and, at this moment,
fear for nothing except the future.

GRÉAGÓIR Ó DÚILL

Born in Dublin in 1946 and raised in Whitehead, Co Antrim, Gréagóir Ó Dúill has a BA from Queen's University, Belfast, an MA in history from UCD and a PhD in English from Maynooth. A professional writer living in Dublin and the Donegal Gaeltacht, he writes mostly in Irish. He has had five collections of verse published and is literary editor of *Comhar*.

Athbhliain

Is é is fearr dúinn anois
(Sneachta an gheimhridh á shéideadh le fórsa)
Cónaí a dhéanamh
Is a dhaingniú in éadan anfa.

Ag deireadh ráithe seo na gile cruálaí
Is na hoighre mailísí, rachaimid an doras amach
Is feicfimid athruithe ar dhreach na tíre
Ar sceach, ar chrann, loch is abhainn, sliabh is coire.

Ní hionann a bheas an tír, dhá cheann an gheimhridh
Is beidh caill ann, eallach is caoirigh, seandaoine
Ach beimid féin ann, athrú orainn mar a gcéanna
Is rachaidh soc an chéachta san ithir bhuan san earrach
    strainséartha.

New Year

Our best plan now
(While the wind lashes the winter snow)
Is to sit tight
And batten down against the storm.

At the end of this month of cruel whiteness
And malicious ice, we will go out the door
And see the changes in the country's appearance
On thorn, tree, lake and river, mountain and corrie.

The country will not be the same at either end of winter
And there will be loss, cattle and sheep, old people
But we will be there, likewise changed
And the plough's snout will enter the enduring earth in the
    unfamiliar spring.

Translated by Aodán Mac Póilin

Geimhreadh

Faoi scáth na díge, fanann an sneachta go mailíseach,
Luíochán ciúin nach n-airím.
Imím go rúitín sa fhliuchlach bhán,
Mo mhéara coise mar leaca oighre ag slupadáil.
Cúlaím faoi shioc-*shock*.
Cuimhním ar lá ar bhris mo bhróg
Tré chabhail bhán chorp caora i ndíog dhorcha eile.
Ligh an samhnas mo fhiacla.
Tá mianach tréasach i ndíoga.
Is mithid fanacht ar an bhóithrín chúng,
Sin nó airdeall síoraí, cos ar an pháipéar scrúdaithe,
Súil le talamh, dall ar gach réalt
Nach mbíonn sioctha i linn oighre.

Winter

In the shelter of the ditch, the snow waits maliciously:
I fail to see the quiet ambush,
Drop ankle-deep in the white wet.
My toes are ice-floes floating
I'm freeze-framed, backing down.
I remember the day my shoe broke
Through the white corpse of a sheep in another ditch —
Nausea licked my teeth.
Ditches have a treacherous quality.
Better to stay on the narrow path,
That, or eternal vigilance, a foot on the examination paper,
Eye to the ground, blind to every star
Not frozen in a pool of ice.

Translated by Aodán Mac Póilin

Don Chonstábla Taca Michael Williams

Amharcann tú orm as páipéar na maidne,
D'aghaidh óg oifigiúil, leathmheangadh ar do bhéal,
Fiaradh beag Piarsach ar do shúil.

Is léir nár shócúil thú faoi
Mhéar in airde an ghrianghrafadóra, ag éisteacht a
    dheabhaidh.
Sin díreach mar atá mo phictiúr féin, ar chomhad.

Lacht forbartha na tíre d'fhuil, dar leo
Ceimiceáin ag claochló cúige,
Prionta deimhnitheach i linn ghlan ghlé.

Maidin Lae Coille, meánoíche scoite,
Do chorp is do chabhail is do chloigeann siabhtha,
Mugshot eile don chomhad.

I dtús do scóir faoi bhláth do chliabh a scaipeadh;
Mo scór faoi bhláth ar fhaire ghoirt sa bhodhránacht.

For Reserve Constable Michael Williams

You look on me from the morning paper,
Your young face official, a faint smile about your mouth,
A slight Pearse-like squint in your eye.

Clearly, you were not at ease beneath
The raised finger of the photographer, his chattering speed —
My own file-photo is just the same.

Your blood, they believe, is a state-developing fluid,
A province-transforming chemical,
Printing clear beneath a bright clear pool.

New Year's morning, midnight behind you,
Body, frame, skull are blown apart,
Another mugshot for the file.

As your twenty years in flower opened, your ribs were
    scattered;
My twenty years in flower but a bitter watch at daybreak.

Translated by Pádraig Mac Fhearghusa

MARY O'MALLEY

Mary O'Malley was born in Connemara and educated at UCG. She lived for eight years in Portugal where she taught English at the New University of Lisbon. She now lives in her native Galway. A member of the organising committee of Cúirt International Poetry Festival, she works as a part-time journalist at UCG. She was shortlisted for the 1989 *Sunday Tribune*/Hennessy Awards. Her first collection is *A Consideration of Silk* (Salmon 1990).

Wordgames
For Oisín

It is not the memory
Of fat dimple knees,
Not the pink puckermouth
Nor the huge blueness
Of my son's eyes
That most mothermoves me,
But the way he took on English
Like an ocean.

A small stumbling Columbus
He stared, thumb rooted in mouth,
Then dipped a toe to test
The light splishy little words.
Soon slithery S words
Were slipping around his tongue:
Elusive eels.

Big angular rocks made him
Heave and puff to adjust
To the ponderous shape of them;
Soon too his mouth stretched

As he shouted fat round sounds.
His caution gone he threw
Hundreds of new words around,
Blowing them like bubbles,
Bouncing them like balls,
Punching the odd recalcitrant word
Such as *thwactor* into shape.

Carwords came quickly.
He reinvented comic talk —
Zoom, pow, yikes and boom.
Weightless, fairy, elf and sprite
Floated from his mouth like blowballs,
Seeming hardly to touch his tongue.

Fire caused him no fear
Because our house then
Had no hearth. But one day
He peered cautiously *under the neath*
At the menacing words that hid
Under the bed at night,
Dark and formless in the gloom,
And even we could not protect him forever
From the dragons of war and death.

Aftermath

For Mike

Last night I looked at you,
A stark man in this grey country
Of short days and long nightfalls.
I watched and marvelled
That you should still be here,
For I had not seen you much
In the storms of these past years.

Time and God and bureaucrats
Have pared us both down
To some of our essentials,
With deft little secateurs
Or blunt edgeless implements,
Such as are sought in murder hunts.

Each inflicted its own pain
As it peeled back, gouged
Or merely hacked away
To reach and reveal a deeper layer,
Here a terra cotta shard
Of smashed solicitude,
There a flint of fear,

Perhaps even a purple thread,
Last remnant of some glorious bolt
Of desire. Such delvings and exhumations
Seldom yield the unbroken,
Though sometimes beautiful tokens
Are taken out of their darkness
To be exposed to the light in museums.

They have left me with furrows
And ridges that no coyness
Can rechristen laughter lines.
Yet you are still here;
And I watching
Wondered if I would ever know
This defined and distant man
That I have lived beside
As I knew the boy
The instant the air shifted between us,
Moments after we met.

Credo

There is a risk
That every consideration of silk,
Each velvet hush between lovers
Is stolen from other women.

That consenting acts of love
Are only enjoyed
Over the staked thighs
Of the unsaved women of El Salvador,

That I have no right
To claim kinship with war women,
Their ripe bellies slit like melons
While I guard

The contentment of my children,
Agonise over which small
Or great talent to nurture,
Which to let die.

But while I am yet free
To observe the rights of womanhood
I will relish and preserve
The sigh, the sway, the night caress

Yes, and the dignity of my children.
I will anoint my wrists with scent,
Fold fine sheets, hoard
Sheer stockings and grow a red rose.

I will hold them all for you
In an inviolate place,
The hallowed nook beside my heart
That no man knows.

Every step I dance
Each glance of love and glistening note
From a golden saxophone
Is an act of faith for I believe

In the resurrection of the damned.
I believe your day
Is an arrow loosed,
It is burning along a silver bow

To meet you rising to your power
Like a crocus in the snow.

CATHAL Ó SEARCAIGH

Cathal Ó Searcaigh, poet and playwright, lives on a small hill farm at the foot of his beloved Mount Errigal in Co Donegal. He is the author of three volumes of verse, the most representative being *Suibhne: Rogha Dánta* (Coiscéim, 1988). *Ag Tnúth leis an tSolas*, his fourth collection, is due from Cló Iar-Chonnachta during 1993. His many quirky, irreverent plays include *Mairimid leis na Mistéirí* and *Tá an Tóin ag Titim as an tSaol*. Twice recipient of Arts Council bursaries, he has also held a number of Poet-in-Residence positions. A popular and persuasive performer of poetry, he has travelled extensively at home and abroad giving readings of his work. A selection of his poetry is available on cassette, *An Bealach 'na Bhaile*, issued by Cló Iar-Chonnachta in 1991. He is currently writer-in-residence at the University of Ulster at Coleraine and Queen's University, Belfast. His latest book is *Homecoming/An Bealach 'na Bhaile*, a bilingual selection of his poems, edited by Gabriel Fitzmaurice and published by Cló Iar-Chonnachta in 1993.

Bó Bhradach

Do Liam Ó Muirthile

D'éirigh sé dúthuirseach déarfainn
den uaigneas a shníonn anuas i dtólamh
fríd na maolchnocáin is fríd na gleanntáin
chomh malltriallach le *hearse* tórraimh;
de bhailte beaga marbhánta na mbunchnoc
nach bhfuil aos óg iontu ach oiread le créafóg;
de na seanlaochra, de lucht roiste na dtortóg
a d'iompaigh an domasach ina deargfhód
is a bhodhraigh é *pink* bliain i ndiaidh bliana
ag éisteacht leo ag maíomh as seanfhóid an tseantsaoil;

de na *bungalows* bheaga bhána atá chomh gránna
le *dandruff* in ascaill chíbeach an Ghleanna;
de na daoine óga gafa i *gcage* a gcinniúna
dálta ainmhithe allta a chaill a ngliceas;
de thrí thrua na scéalaíochta i dtruacántas
lucht na dífhostaíochta, den easpa meanmna,
den iargúltacht, den chúngaigeantacht ar dhá thaobh an
    Ghleanna;
de na leadhbacha breátha thíos i dTigh Ruairí
a chuir an fear ag bogadaigh ann le fonn
ach nach dtabharfadh túrálú ar a raibh de shú ann;

de theorainneacha treibhe, de sheanchlaíocha teaghlaigh,
de bheith ag mún a mhíshástachta in éadan na mballaí
a thóg cine agus creideamh thart air go teann.
D'éirigh sé dúthuirseach de bheith teanntaithe sa Ghleann
is le rúide bó bradaí maidin amháin earraigh
chlearáil sé na ballaí is *hightailáil* anonn adaí.

A Braddy Cow

For Liam Ó Muirthile

He got fed-up, I'd swear,
of the loneliness that constantly seeps down,
through the rolling hills, through the valleys
sluggish as a hearse;
of the lazy hamlets of the foothills
empty of youth as of earth;
of the old warriors, of the sodbusters
who turned to red-sod the peaty soil
and who deafened him pink, year-in, year-out,
bragging of the old sods of the past;

of the small, white bungalows ugly
as dandruff in the sedgy headlands of the Glen;
of the young trapped in the cage of their fate
like wild animals who have lost their cunning;
of the three sorrows of storytelling in the misery
of the unemployed, of low spirits,
of the backwardness, of the narrowmindedness of both
    sides of the Glen,
of the fine birds below in Ruairi's
who stirred the man in him
but who couldn't care less about his lusting;

of tribal boundaries, of ancient household ditches,
of pissing his frustration at race and religion
that walled him in.
He got fed up of being fettered in the Glen
and, bucking like a braddy cow one spring morning,
he cleared the walls and hightailed away.

               Translated by Gabriel Fitzmaurice

MICHEAL O'SIADHAIL

Micheal O'Siadhail was born in Dublin in 1947. He has been a lecturer at Trinity College, Dublin, and a professor at the Dublin Institute for Advanced Studies and is now a full-time poet. He has published seven collections of poetry. His latest book is *Hail! Madam Jazz: New and Selected Poems* (Bloodaxe 1993). He has read his poetry widely in Ireland, Britain and North America.

In a New York Shoe Shop

Canned blues rhythms hum the background.
Air-conditioned from the swelter, a choosy
clientele vets the canted wall-racks

Of new-look summer shoes. Unbargained for,
a handsome inky coloured man catching
the snappy syncopation, jazzes across the floor

to proof-dance a pair of cream loafers.
Beaming, he bobs and foot-taps; pleased
with his purchase, he jives a short magnificat.

A friend from Maryland had once described
seeing in his grandfather's cellar the rusted irons
that had fettered a chain-gang of black slaves.

Behind the polyrhythm, the scoops, the sliding
pitches and turns, I hear the long liquid line
of transcended affliction; women with gay

kerchiefs are prayer-hot in the praise-house
or whoop in Alabama's cotton-fields. Life ad-libs
with a jug and washboard; sublimity forgives.

In submission to the pulse this customer lets go,
swings low to the bitter-sweet quadruple
time, unmuzzled, human and magnificent.

Visionary

What was it then, what commanded such ardour?
A scattering of lonely islands, a few gnarled
seaboard townlands, underworld of a language frail
as patches of snow hiding in the shadows of a garden.

But the dwindling were so living. In this wonderland
of might-have-been I fell for the rhythm, the undertone
of my father's speech, built a golden dream.
(As you dreamt that land was falling asunder.)

A world as it is or a world as we want it:
when to resist old fate's take-for-granted
or when to submit; had I known before I slid
into a snowy fantasy, a fairyland of squander ....

Was it a lavishness, a hankering for self-sacrifice,
part arrogance, part the need of the twice
shy for a paradise of the ideal, pure and beyond,
where one man's will turns a hag to a princess.

Oh I was the fairy story's third son, the one
who, unlike his elder brothers would not shun
a hag by the roadside: surely I'd rub the ring,
summon a sword of light to slay the dragon.

Tell me now that land was a last outpost,
a straggling from another time no one's utmost
could save; the hungry beast of change roved
nearer, that vision was a ghost dance with the past.

Tell me now third brothers too have grown
older, have even learned to smile at highflown
dreams. Then tell me still somewhere in the thaw
a child is crying over a last island of snow.

Stranger

A youngster I came, pilgrim to the source;
fables of a native bliss stirred mottoes:
a land without a tongue, a land without a soul.
As the currachs drew alongside the steamer
men in dark blue shirts shouted exotic words.

In the kitchen a daughter returned on holiday
switches from her mother's tongue to chide
her London children. As I listen it seems
I am foreign to both, neither fish nor flesh.
Was I to be a stranger in this promised land?

I slip into a glove of language. But there's still
a vividness, an older mood, small courtesies
to fortune: the sea must have its own — to swim
is to challenge fate. Child of reason and will
I am at most a sojourner in that mind.

Talk then of the mainland as *the world outside*,
enter and become a citizen of this stony room:
handkerchief fields claimed from rocks, dung
dried for fuel, unmortared boulder walls,
calfskin shoes, stark artifices of survival.

A widower welcomes my visits, opens his sorrow
to the incomer. Gauchely, I mention his loneliness:
Hadn't he his turn? ask two neighbour women
swirling their petticoats *What ails him?*
they banter, standing in the sunshaft of a doorway.

One evening on the flags dancing starts up;
no music, island women summering from Boston
lilt reels, long to be courted. But men
shy of plaid skirts or lipstick don't dare
(still too boyish, subtleties pass me by).

Nudges and smothered laughter among the men.
Over again the word *stranger*. I bridle,
yearn to be an insider, unconsciously begin
a changeling life; turning a live-in lover
I wear my second nature, a grafted skin.

Questing

A time for gaiety, a time to sunder
taken-for-granted gods, to flounder
or squander; a feckless valley-time
before we find a cause and climb
into the laps of countergods, a bizarre
time when in some Dublin bar,
arguing the toss as best we could,
we served our apprentice adulthood.

Till closing time we talked and talked;
the intellect now cock of the walk.
What does it mean? We interrogate
our upbringing, unravelling with apostate
zeal a web of code and token
and court our guilty ecstasy of broken
symbols, a dance along the precipice,
new and giddy pull of the abyss.

We leave, carrying our parcels of beer
across a sidestreet; someone for the sheer
hell heaves a brick at a windowpane —
we scuttle out of trouble down a lane
back to our meagre Bohemia to expound
meanings of the universe. Above the sound
of our voices a bedsitter radio is playing;
between stations, a blurred music sways.

Nead

Déan síoriontas de mhíorúilte seo na neide
A dhlúthaíonns soip na páirte ina ngaol;
Ach dlí an áil é fáil faoi réir le greadadh
Idir chorp, chleite is sciathán amach.

De chrann ariamh orainn tréiscint na treibhe,
Séanadh na neide is an fháinneáil linn féin,
Ní éan aonchleite aríst é do dheartháir
Éan corr feasta í an deirfiúr is dílse.

Tá an reacht i gcrích. Fiú dhár mbuíochas
Ní túisce anois lucht aon áil cruinn
Ná ar éigin na seansíomálacha ceilte
Ag gobaireacht is cocaireacht éadmhar na neide.

Bíodh sé de phláinéad orthu, bíodh sé le fánaíocht,
Deargstrainséaraí dhá chéile a rinne an nead;
Brioscacht na neide féin a chruthaigh an buanadas —
An misneach a dhlúthaigh, an misneach a scar.

Nest

Marvel at the work of this nest:
love-straws kneaded into kin;
still the nest's law is to scatter
feather and wing, one and all.

We're born to betray the nest,
to quit the brood, flutter alone:
brothers no longer of a feather,
sisters already lone travellers.

And so it is. In spite of ourselves,
no sooner now the tribe together
than all the nestling sores lurk,
we're rivals in the peck and chatter.

Star-guided or even by chance,
blank strangers gathered this nest;
its frailty still its own fail-safe:
daring to gather is daring to scatter.

Translated by the author

Nugent

Meandar cuidsúlach, puth as aer,
Nóiméad é as nuaíocht an lae
Ag léimt thar lampa draíocht
Na teilifíse — an príosúnach.
Th'éis dhá bhliain is naoi mí
Saoradh an príosúnach Nugent inniu
As géibheann na Cise Fada.
             A Thiarna, ab í
An scéin ag damhsa ina shúile a bhain
Dhár lúdracha muid?
             Leanadh don stair:
Le scéal eile as Nicearagua
An rása deiridh as Nás na Rí.
Cén spás atá ag nuaíocht nó ag stair?

Mar sin é. Amáireach feicfear
A pheictiúr ar leithmhilliún páipéar:
Nugent an príosúnach a saoradh inné.
Amáireach tá an seomra thiar le réiteach.

Is amhlaidh a clúdaíodh a shamhail
Le scuaid den phéint.
Cén chúis is fiú snig fola
Gan trácht ar bhláth na hóige;
Le cúrsaí reatha an anama an ceol.

'Sea, cé a bhí i Nugent?
Máirtíreach as an ísealtír
Coipthe ag cúis is ag cearta
Cromtha faoina dhá bhliain fhichead.
Fós in uafás shúile Nugent
Siúileann an saighdiúr singil deiridh
Stiúgtha, stróicthe i ndiaidh Napoleon;
Is 'chuile chúlmhuintir ariamh ag spágáil,
Ag cúitiú dhúinne ár gcompóirte,
Thrí fhearann fuar na staire.
Ab iad a shúile glórach féin
A chuir an scéin seo ionainn?

Nugent

Eyecatching jiffy, whiff from the sky,
a moment from the news of the day
darts over the television's
magic lamp — the prisoner.
Two years nine months after

prisoner Nugent today released
from Long Kesh camp.
                              God
was it fright's dance in the eyes
unhinged us?
                              History continued:
from Nicaragua a news story,
the last race from Naas.
What space has news or history?

That's the way. Tomorrow will see
on a half million newspapers his picture.
Nugent the prisoner yesterday freed.
Tomorrow the backroom must be put in order.

Actually his image was covered over
by a spatter of paint.
What cause is worth a tint of blood
not to mind the bloom of youth;
to the soul's current affairs belongs music.

Yes, who was Nugent?
A martyr from the netherland
feverish with cause and dues
stooped under twenty two years.
but in the fear of Nugent's eye
walks the last private soldier
famished, bedraggled after Napoleon;
all camp followers who ever tramped,
smarting for our comfort,
across the cold land of history.
Were those his own crazed eyes
who terrified us so?

Translated by the author

PÁDRAIG Ó SNODAIGH

Born in Carlow in 1935, Pádraig Ó Snodaigh is director of the publishing house Coiscéim. Among his publications are three books of poetry in Irish (one of which has been translated into Italian), works of history, *Hidden Ulster* and *Comhghuadlaithe na Réabhlóide*, and two novellas, *Rex* and *Linda*, both in Irish. He has also translated two books from Italian (poetry and a novel).

---

as *Ó Pharnell go Queenie*

2.

Paris

Pictiúirí díot níl agam anois
Níor choinníos an beagán d'fhág tú liom:
nótaí .... dornán beag de phíosaí ....
iad ag tanú go púdar ar an imeall
ag teip
ar rianta salaithe a bhfillte.

Ach bíonn tú romham
ar nós an fhocail riachtanach úd a bhíonns ar bhior do
bhéil
is ná tagann chugat
— féachaint áirithe ar aghaidheanna
a chasann ceann go fiosrach
.... cá bhfaca san cheana?
cé uirthi?
do ghuth ag bean amháin
do shiúl áit eile
.... an fuadar oscailte dorais.
.... an hata síos ar clé

243

do mhuinéal romham, do chúl,
do lámha ag ardú cupa.
I bpíosaí tá tú,
ag síothlú uaim
ag imeacht mar fhaobhar ó ghloine
i síon na mara.

Is smaoiníos .... nach amhlaidh
le taisí na naomh,
fiacal leis siúd,
éadaí dá cuid, ciarsúir, peann leis siúd eile.

Is smaoiníos leis gur taise díot mé,
mo chuid gruaige trínar shnigh do mhéaracha
mo bheola ar ar luigh do bhéal

Níor thitis i lóipíní bána do litreacha
a stracas ar an b*Pont Neuf*.
Níor shloig an abhainn tú 'na dteannta san.
Fanann tú fad a fhanaim-se.

7.

Steyning

Do roinnfinn deas agus clé leat,
thuas agus thíos,
a raibh is a bheas.
Bhlaisfinn do dheora
mar a bhlaisim do phóga.
Iomlán mo bheo.
Iomlán mo bheatha-sa.
Roinnim áilleacht leat,
áthas do-shamhlaithe,
aoibhneas nár shíleas ann,

sonas, sástacht, suaimhneas
ar ar chuala trácht
ar léas fúthu,
nárbh ann dóibh riamh dom
ach leat-sa, *lady*.

Do roinnfinn deas leat is clé
mar a roinneadh thuas agus thíos.
Roinnfinn lár leat is íoghar
is an íoghar chun an láir.
Do roinnfinn dubh leat is bán
mar a roinn muid liath, glas is gorm.

Do roinnfinn do bhuairt leat a stór.
Do roinnfinn do bhrón
mar a roinn muid binn agus buaic
nár shíleas bheith ann.

Do roinnfinn lá leat is oíche
Roinnim a bhfuil leat mo mhian
— go roinntear a bhfuil romhainn —
Roinn liom do bhuairt, roinn liom do bhrón
is fearrde ár ngrá é is doimhne dár searc.

Roinnfinn dubh leat is bán
clé, deas, bun agus barr.
Roinnfinn mo shaol leat.
Roinntear ár ngrá.
Ná ceil do bhuairt orm, ná ceil do bhrón;
Níor cheileamar aoibhneas,
níor cheileamar grá.

Éire a ghéillfinn duit, *Kate*
más rí di mé féin
is an féin sin do ghéillfinn,

nó a bhfuil de ag sruthlú tríom-sa go fóill
ag macallú.

An oiread is féidir
géillim
ós tú mé anois
ó thumas d'aon léim chugat, ionat
is an léimt sin chomh céillí
go mbím buíoch de de shíor
is díot-sa, m'eangach tarrthála
is ded fháilte
mo líon, lón, lán.
Éire a ghéillim
is mé
inniu as inné
anois, *Kate*, duitse, go buan.

14.

An mbeadh sé níos éasca duit
dá ndéarfainn nach raibh grá ann a thuilleadh
is a fhágaint fútsa beartú dá réir,
mé a mhealladh dá mb'fhiú leat,
cúl a thabhairt dom dá mb'fhearr duit;
An mbeadh sé níos éasca duit
diúltú duit féin is gan mé ann,
mise a fhágaint fúm féin ....

Fuascailt an scéil sin ní bheidh ann
nó ní thriailfead-sa é. Ní leomhfainn
ar eagla do ghortaithe
meandar inste na bréige
a d'aithneofá ach ráite
ós eol duit-se, a stór, a ghlanmhalairt.

26.

Katherine, a stór (1891)

Réabtar domhain
Bristear is bactar
Tógtar ó chéile iad
Lobhann, crapann
Seirgíonn isteach iontu féin
Leagtar

Is samhlaím
fórsaí is láidre fós á mbrú
sliotair idir chamánaibh na nDéithe
amach anseo

Ach anois
agus anfa ag amhastraíl lasmuigh
ná bí lag laistigh a chroí liom
bí liom tóg uaim mar a thógaim uait
as dásacht díse tiocfam tríd

Fianna sa chró
is éasca dóibh más beirt
cúl le cúl, aonad
ag faire dá chéile

Sleánna teilgthe
á sraonadh go dtí
nach léir
as éascaíocht alta an aonaid
an aon iad an bheirt

Is beirt muid. Is aon.
Is maíonn toil is mian

Go dtiocfam tríd
Is tiocfam
    tiocfam
     tiocfam
     tríd
      mar aon
     mar dís
mé is tú.

from *From Parnell to Queenie*

2.

Paris

I have no pictures of you now
I didn't keep the few you left me:
notes .... a handful of scraps ....
fraying to powder at the edges
fading
on the age-stained folds.

But you are always before me
like that apt word on the tip of the tongue
that doesn't come
— a certain expression on faces
that turn the inquisitive head
.... where did I see that before?
on whom?
your voice with one woman
your walk with another
.... the flurry of an entrance
.... the hat askew
your neck before me, your back,
your hands raising a cup.
You are vanishing
bit by bit
like broken glass smoothed
in the roll of the sea.

And I thought .... isn't it the same
with the relics of the saints,

a tooth here,
this one's clothes, that one's handkerchief, yet
   another's pen.

And then I realized that I'm a relic of you,
my hair you ran your fingers through
my lips where you laid your mouth.

You didn't fall with the white flakes of your letters
I tore up on the *Pont Neuf.*
The river didn't swallow you along with them.
You last while I do.

7.

   Steyning

Right and left I'd share with you,
above and below,
what was and will be.
I'd taste your tears
as I savour your kisses.
The whole of my being.
The whole of my life.
I share beauty with you,
happiness beyond imagining,
sweetness I never thought existed,
happiness, contentment, peace
I'd heard about,
that I never knew
lady, but with you.

With you I'd share right and left,
up and down.
Centre and edge I'd share with you,

outside-inside.
I'd share black and white with you
as we shared grey, green and blue.

I'd share your troubles, love.
I'd share your lows
as we shared heights
I never thought existed.

I'd share day and night with you
I share what is my hope
— may we share what is to come —
Share your troubles with me, your sorrows,
all the better our love for it, all the deeper.

I'd share black and white,
left, right, bottom and top.
I'd share my life with you.
May our love, too, be shared.
Don't hide your trouble from me, your sorrow;
We didn't conceal our delight
nor our love.

I'd surrender Ireland for you, *Kate*,
even if I myself were King
and that same self surrender
and whatever courses through me yet
echoing.

As much as possible
I surrender
now that you are I
since I dived to you, into you,
a leap so wise
that I'm ever grateful for it

and to you, net of my recovery
and to your welcome
my net, my sustenance, my fill.
Ireland I'd surrender
and myself
today out of yesterday
the present, *Kate*, for you, forever.

14.

Would it be easier for you
if I said that love was dead
and to leave it up to you
to woo me if you thought 'twas worth it,
to rebuff me if you preferred;
Would it be easier for you
to deny yourself in my absence,
leaving me to myself ....

No resolution to that will be found
since I won't put it to the test. I wouldn't dare
for fear of hurting you
in the instant of the saying of the lie
you'd easily recognize
knowing, love, as you do that the opposite is true.

26.

Katherine, my love (1891)

Worlds are rent
Broken and blocked
Torn asunder
They shrink, rot

Waste into themselves
Are knocked

    And I imagine
still stronger forces smashing
sliotars between the hurleys of the Gods
later on

    But now
with a storm barking outside
don't weaken, love,
be with me, take from me as I take from you
coupled in audacity we'll pull through

    Fianna in testing-pits
find it easier if paired
back to back as one
protecting each other

    Deflecting the spears
until it's not clear
from their acrobatic union
if the two are one

We are two. Are one.
Desire and will declare
We will pull through
And we'll pull through
    pull through
     pull through
    as one
    as two
me and you.

Translated by Gabriel Fitzmaurice

DERRY O'SULLIVAN

Born in Bantry in 1944, Derry O'Sullivan studied Latin and Philosophy at University College Cork and took further studies in Paris and Stockholm. A former Capuchin priest, he is now married to Jean and has three children. Awards include an Arts Council Bursary and four Oireachtas awards, notably the Seán Ó Ríordáin memorial. His collection *Cá Bhfuil do Iúdas?* was published by Coiscéim in 1989. He has lived in Paris since 1969 and teaches at the Sorbonne, Institut Catholique de Paris and Institut Electronique de Paris.

Marbhghin 1943: Glaoch ar Liombó

(do Nuala McCarthy)

Saolaíodh id bhás thú
is cóiríodh do ghéaga gorma
ar chróchar beo do mháthar
sreang an imleacáin slán eadraibh
amhail líne ghutháin as ord.
Dúirt an sagart go rabhais ródhéanach
don uisce baiste rónaofa
a d'éirigh i Loch Bó Finne
is a ghlanadh fíréin Bheanntraí.
Gearradh uaithi thú
is filleadh thú gan ní
i bpáipéar *Réalt an Deiscirt*
cinnlínte faoin gCogadh Domhanda le do bhéal.
Deineadh comhrainn duit de bhosca oráistí
is mar *requiem* d'éist do mháthair
le casúireacht amuigh sa phasáiste
is an bhanaltra á rá léi
go raghfá gan stró go Liombó.
Amach as Ospidéal na Trócaire
d'iompair an garraíodóir faoina ascaill thú

254

i dtafann gadhar de shochraid
go gort neantógach
ar a dtugtar fós an Coiníneach.

Is ann a cuireadh thú
gan phaidir, gan chloch, gan chrois
i bpoll éadoimhin i dteannta
míle marbhghin gan ainm
gan de chuairteoirí chugat ach na madraí ocracha.
Inniu, daichead bliain níos faide anall,
léas i *Réalt an Deiscirt*
nach gcreideann diagairí a thuilleadh
gur ann do Liombó.
Ach geallaimse duit, a dheartháirín
nach bhfaca éinne dath do shúl,
nach gcreidfead choíche iontu arís:
tá Liombó ann chomh cinnte is atá Loch Bó Finne
agus is ann ó shin a mhaireann do mháthair,
a smaointe amhail neantóga á dó
gach nuachtán ina leabhar urnaí,
ag éisteacht le leanaí neamhnite
i dtafann tráthnóna na madraí.

Stillborn 1943: A Call to Limbo

You were born dead
And your blue limbs were arranged
On your mother's live bier —
Umbilical cord still intact,
An out-of-order telephone line.
The priest said you were too late
For the blessed baptismal water
Which flowed from Milky Way Lake

To anoint the faithful of Bantry.
You were cut from her
And folded unwashed
In a copy of the *Southern Star,*
World War headlines pressed to your lips.
They made a coffin for you from an orangebox
And your mother listened to the requiem
Hammering in the corridor
As the nurses assured her
That you were a dead cert for Limbo.
Out the gate of the Mercy Hospital
The gardener carried you under one arm —
A funeral of dogs barked with you
All the way to a patch of nettles
Called the Rabbit Warren.

There you were buried
Without prayer nor stone nor cross
In a shallow hole alongside
A thousand other stillborn babies —
The hungry dogs waited.
Today, forty years later,
I read in the *Southern Star*
That theologians no longer
Believe in Limbo.
But believe me, little brother,
Whose pupil never saw the light,
When I say to Hell with them all:
Limbo exists as certainly as Milky Way Lake
And it's there your mother lives,
Her thoughts burning her like nettles,
Every newspaper a prayer book
As she listens for unwashed babies
In the evening bark of dogs.

Translated by Michael Davitt

Foighne
(Tráthnóna Geimhridh ag feitheamh leat)

An teach ina thost
Mar oíche le hord
An cat ina luí
Mar chogar faoin mbord;
Beola an linbh
Faoi eochair le suan;
An lampa sa chúinne
Mar ghealach ar chuan;
An scáileán mar phóca
A chuardaíonn bacach;
An leabharlann ag feitheamh
Mar chrann le hEarrach;

Guthán ar an urlár
Mar ghadaí ar chroch;
Ticeáil an chloigín
Ag titim mar chloch;
Cathaoir le fuinneog
Mar ghadhar ag an uaigh;
An páipéar ag fanacht
Le péarlaí an dúigh;
'S mise mar mharmar
Ag tnúth le siséal;
Mar chapall ag satailt
Is srian ar a bhéal;

Mar chruit atá gléasta
Ag cláirseoir gan mhéar;
Mar smólach i gcliabhán
A chanann go géar;
Mar othar faoi allas
Ag taibhreamh ar phiolla;

257

Mar fhile gan mheabhair
A shantaíonn an siolla —
Éistim le céim
Chun an staighre a mhúscailt
Mar orgánaí a thagann
Chun nótaí a fhuascailt;

As tarraiceán boird
Tógaim pictiúr
De chnoc Chill Iníon,
Mar, le súile ceiliúir,
D'itheamar áille
Oileán Dheilg Inis
A cheangail na manaigh
Le slabhraí an tinnis;
Do thógas do lámh
Ag féachaint go humhal
Ar phríosúnach a dhamhsaigh
I gcealla do shúl.

Ach an teach ina thost
'S an oíche faoin mbord
Fanaim mar mhanach
Ag satailt ar ord;
Le méara an allais
Cuardaím mar bhacach
I bpócaí an Gheimhridh
Blúirín den Earrach;
Ar mharmar an uaignis
Le peann mar shiséal
Múnlaím do bheola
Ag ól as buidéal;
Má thriallair abhaile
Roimh phiolla an lae
Cuirfear mo chosa
Ar meisce le spré.

Anois i bPáras,
Bús gluaisteán 's bus,
Labhrann tú fúm
Le ceiliúradh do chos;
Beidh clocha an fheithimh
Mar ualach neamhní
Nuair a fheicim an doras
Ag oscailt im chroí;
Nuair a rinceann tú chugam
Mar chogar gealaí
Beidh guthán na croiche
Mar ghadhar ag gáirí;
Má ghlacann tú uaimse
Péarlaí an dúigh
Réabfad na slabhraí
Chun léimt as an uaigh.

Patience

An abbey the house,
A finger on lips,
A chair for a cot
The cat on sleep sips;
The face of the child
Lies swaddled in dreams
Like moonbeams in brooks
The lamp sews night's seams;
The flickering screen
Like a tramp's torn bag,
Nostalgic for Spring
The pine bookshelves sag;
The ticks of the clock
Like thieves on the loose;

The phone on the floor,
Its neck in a noose;
Each window a hole
Where dogs whine for drink;
The blank page awaits
A necklace of ink.

And cold marble I
Impatient for steel,
A stallion's mad prance
With manacled heel;
A harp tightly strung
For fingerless play
A thrush in a cage,
Its warble dismay.
The sweat of the sick,
No needle, no pill;
Amnesia prone
I rhyme pill with nil.
I wait for her step
To startle the stairs;
Her requiem soon
Will coffin my cares.
I open a drawer,
I fondle a view
Of Killiney hill
Where trysting with you
I ate of the fast
In Dalkey's sea cell
Brown friars there in chains
Linked heaven and hell.
Taking your hand,
I stared in surprise,
A manacled monk
I danced in your eyes.

But
The house sips from night,
An abbey its chair,
A monk I remain
In prancing despair;
My fingers of sweat,
A tramp seeking alms,
Poke winter's torn bag
For crumbs of Spring calms;
In marbled retreat,
A pen for my steel,
I chisel your lips
With Bacchic appeal;
If you should return
Before Dawn's poor pill,
My feet will carouse
On Ecstasy's hill.
In Paris, above
The snarling of cars,
I hear your light feet
In tune with the stars;
The thieves of delay
Like bearers of joy
Will open the door
And patience destroy.
When towards me you run,
A whisper of moon,
The phone in its noose
At nightholes will croon.
If you should accept
This necklace of ink,
I'll burst lonely chains
And dance on Death's brink.

Translated by the author

GABRIEL ROSENSTOCK

Born in 1949, Gabriel Rosenstock is Chairman of *Poetry Ireland/Éigse Éireann*, an honorary life member of the Irish Translators' Association and a member of the Irish Writers' Union and British Haiku Society. Publications include *Portrait of the Artist as an Abominable Snowman* (Forest Books, UK), *Oráistí* (Cló Iar-Chonnachta) and erotic haiku, *Cold Moon* (Brandon 1993). Among the authors he has translated into Irish are Alarcón, Heaney, Roggeman and Grass.

Tóraíocht

I

Cá bhfuil na dánta a gheallas
A scríobhfainn duit?
Nílid i ndúch —
Gheobhair iad i gcúr aibhneacha
I bhfarraigí
I ngal os cionn failltreacha
Ina nguairneáin gaoithe
I súile fiolar
Sna scamaill
Sna spéartha
Fiú sna réalta.
Táid ar a gcúrsa síoraí
Ó neamhní go neamhní.
Nílid i gcló —
Sciob cumhracht bláthanna iad
Is tú ar do ghogaide sa ghairdín,
Ghoin neantóga iad
Chuimil copóga iad
Thuirling bóiní Dé orthu
Is shiúil go criticiúil
Ag cuardachríme is meadarachta
Gan teacht ar theideal fiú.

Ní féidir tú a ainmniú!
Gairim thú ó lá go lá
Le gach anáil.
Cá bhfuil na briathra?
Ghlacais chugat féin iad.
Na haidiachtaí?
Neadaíonn id bhrollach geal.
Poncaíocht?
Tá tú maisithe aici,
Ainmfhocail, gutaí is consain,
Nathanna uile na Gaeilge
Tiomnaím duit iad — 'Eithne!

II

Ó aois go haois lorgaím do chló
I m'eite
Im dhuilleog,
Nuair is leanaí sinn
Laochra,
Seanóirí,
Ar lic an bháis
Is fiú sa bhroinn
Tá gach nóiméad le saol na saol
Ag ullmhú dom dhánsa duit —
Ag cur fáilte romhat.
An gcloisir gála?
Casann an domhan
Casann gach ní
Casann na cnoic is na sléibhte.
Dhúnamar, d'osclaíomar ár súile
Is dhún arís le hiontas.

III

Ná beannaigh dom
Ná féach orm

263

Ná lorg mé
Táim ar mo theitheadh
Ad lorg
Ní hann dúinn
Áit ar bith
Am ar bith,
Nílimid i bhfriotal
Nílimid i ngrá
(Dá dhéine ár ngrá dá chéile).
Beir ar lámh orm,
A chuisle; éist le tiompán an chroí
A bhuail dúinn anallód,
Ní thuigimid fós a bhrí.

The Search

for my wife, Eithne

I

Where are the poems I promised
I would write for you?
They are not in ink —

You will find them in the foam of rivers
In the seas
In the vapour above clifftops
In the swirling breeze
In eagles' eyes
In the clouds
In the skies
Even in the stars.
They're on their eternal journey
From void to void.
They are not in print —

The flowers' sweetness snatched them
While you hunkered in the garden.
Nettles burned them
Dock soothed them
Ladybirds landed on them
And walked like critics
Seeking rhyme and metre.
They even failed to find a title. For who
Could put a name on you!
And yet each day I name you
With every breath.
Where are all the verbs?
You have gathered them to yourself.
The adjectives?
Nestling in your breast.
Punctuation?
It adorns you.
Nouns, vowels, consonants,
The Irish language, its sound and sense,
I dedicate to you, Eithne.

II

From age to age I seek your shape
Like a winglet
Like a leaf.
When we are children,
Heroes,
and elders,
On death's cold stone
And in the womb,
Every moment
Shapes my poem —
It ever welcomes you.
Can you hear the gale?
The world turns

And all is turning,
The hills and the peaks above them.
We closed our eyes, and opened them,
Then closed them again in wonder.

III

Do not greet me
Do not look at me
Do not seek me
I escape
I seek you
We do not exist
In any time
In any place
We are not in the realms of words
Or love
(Although our love is strong).
Take my hand,
Love; hear the heart's tympany
That beat long ago for you and me,
That we still don't understand.

Translated by Gabriel Fitzmaurice

Billie Holiday

D'fháiscis pian
As sárbhinneas
Binneas
As sárphian
Nuair a éigníodh thú in aois
Do dheich mbliana duit
B'in an chéad tairne

I gcéasadh do chine is do bhanúlachta
Is d'ealaíne
Go dtí sa deireadh
Gur scanraigh do ghuth féin tú,
A ainnir i sról.

Billie Holiday

You squeezed pain
From the height of sweetness
Sweetness
From the height of pain
When you were raped
At ten years old
That was the first nail
In the crucifixion of your race, your womanhood
And your art
Till in the end
Your own voice frightened you
Lady in satin.

Translated by Gabriel Fitzmaurice

Teilifís
(faoi m'iníon Saffron)

Ar a cúig a chlog ar maidin
Theastaigh an teilifís uaithi.
An féidir argóint le beainín
Dhá bhliain go leith?

Síos linn le chéile
Níor bhacas fiú le gléasadh
Is bhí an seomra préachta.
Gan solas fós sa spéir
Stánamar le hiontas ar scáileán bán.
Anois! Sásta?
Ach chonaic sise sneachta
Is sioráf tríd an sneachta
Is ulchabhán Artach
Ag faoileáil
Os a chionn.

Television

(for my daughter Saffron)

At five o'clock in the morning
She wanted television.
Who can argue with a little woman
Two and a half years old?
Down we went together
I didn't even dress
And the room was freezing.
No light yet in the sky
We stared in wonder at the white screen.
Happy now?
But she saw snow
And a giraffe through it
And an arctic owl
Wheeling
Above it.

Translated by Gabriel Fitzmaurice

anois

anois tá gach ní slán,
cá bhfios an mbeidh arís go brách?
blais nóiméad seo an ghrásta —
taoi arís id naíonán fásta.

now

now everything is well,
will it ever be again?
take this moment, then, and taste —
man again a child of grace.

Translated by Gabriel Fitzmaurice

sliabh

an bhfuil na sléibhte gorm dubh nó bán?
an bhfuil siad le feiscint go hiomlán?
an bhfaca daonnaí sliabh
riamh?

mountain

are the mountains blue, black, white?
are they translatable by sight?
was a mountain ever seen
by a human being?

Translated by Gabriel Fitzmaurice

DEIRDRE SHANAHAN

Deirdre Shanahan lives and works in London where she has published a volume of poetry, *Legal Tender*, for which she received an Eric Gregory Award. She writes for the stage and her play *Prussian Blue* was broadcast on RTE in 1991.

Thresholds

My mother visiting
prepared food,
floured hands flying over pastry
she tucked down memories
returning to her grandmother
in a new plunge of thought.

She spoke of Sarah
standing at Bulls Mouth,
the water's edge,
gleaning from English soldiers
garrisoned in the West
the signs I write now.

Sarah found a self in words;
wrote for the villagers
to the landlord,
securing homes and pastures
through fine sweeps and curves
in the tide of years.

Distant from her house,
unused in such strength
I lack tension now, need skill;
émigrée, crafting
like driftwood on waves
dipping and gone.

Letters Home

The nurse in the night leaves Euston.
It is late and could be dangerous,
policemen mingle doorways,
patrol street corners from wooden huts.

In her travelling suit she meanders,
crosses the squares, her own cartographer,
to the nurses' home
in South London.

No sirens, taxis or buses,
instead the policeman on duty
who offers to carry her case
across the city and Chelsea Bridge.

Her mother's warnings
accumulate dust on the dresser.
She has written that she is safe
and there is always the underground,

but remembers one bomb near the hospital,
it cracked from the sky and broke glass,
everyone carried mattresses outside;
details omitted in letters home.

Their version is of parties and dances,
complimentary tickets, the plays she has seen
and her brother across the river
who visits on Sundays.

Land

Visiting my father's village
we walked along his field
rented out to a neighbour
whose cattle kept the grass down.
We heard how great-grandfather
returned from gold-prospecting
and bought the land.

Each step on the ridges
was a kind of pilgrimage,
a way of paying respects,
until things changed.
Cows splayed,
the defining path was overgrown
and my father was forced to sell.

At a distance of miles
in his untidy garden of plants
my father turns the soil
with a hurt unhurried eye.
I see strangers work the land,
want to run there so hard
and not come back.

Intricate thoughts come
to a bending brow
as I write six years on
since moving from Wales
where birds twitched the telegraph lines
and he consumed words.

Leaning against the pink wall
on the mantelshelf, a postcard
of an old man looks out
from the edges, to this world,
angling fingers, steady as chapel walls,
around a cigarette,

reminding me of a cottager
caught in ropes,
lapsing for risks in valleys,
climbing in mist waves
and oceans of endless air,
a voice in resonance and fall,

a handler of words
whose pen wields weight,
ink black as December
carrying thoughts
like a curragh
on a heady sea to the shore.

JOE SHEERIN

Joe Sheerin was born in 1941 in Dargoon — a pre-medieval but impossible to leave behind townland — in Co Leitrim. His work was published in *Poetry Dimensions* (Faber 1982). His collection *A Crack in the Ice* was published by Dolmen Press in 1985.

A True Story

No blacks, no Irish, no dogs.
I read the rooms to let near
Gloucester Road, brushed my hackles
Flat and continued my search. Then

It wasn't the jibe of race but
The spot between black and dog.
My blood burned and my thick
Tongue filled my gob, blocking the
Words of release, black Irish dog.

I found a room, a den between two
Floors, a curtain to draw behind
And a bed for the neutral night. I
Found love too, more than my ire deserved.
She poured ointment on my tongue. I
Lapped affection, licked kisses on her face.

The dogs were rehabilitated first. The
Blacks legalised on penny postcards on shop
Fronts. I trimmed my words for the Anglo-
Saxon ear. Nothing remains but a green

Passport. Recently on returning from Paris
A customs official, concerned about rabies,
Asked if I were bringing in a dog.

KNUTE SKINNER

Knute Skinner lives in Killaspuglonane, Co Clare, and spends part of the year teaching at Western Washington University in America. His most recent book is *The Bears and Other Poems* from Salmon Publishing.

The Back of his Neck

Sitting at the window of my study,
I see Dunstan, seventeen years old,
walk into the yard.

So.
At eleven twenty-nine he's finally
risen from bed.

He stands for a moment
examining the ground.
He is selecting an appropriate spot
to pee.

I wonder if he's sorry he slept so late.
Edna and Morgan have ridden their bikes to town,
and I have finished, at last,
a difficult poem.

I see the back of his neck
and then his ears
as if for the first time.
His haircut does make
one hell of a difference.

Turning back to the house, he looks in my window,
notes with surprise that I am looking at him,
sticks out his tongue, then smiles.

It isn't known
how much I love him.

Manure Bags

The country roads are replete
with empty manure bags.
Whitish grey in the dark, they
confront those travellers
who walk out in the night
from farm to farm.
They seem at first a vision
of something else:
 a body slumped in grass
at the edge of tyre tracks
— no, more likely a dog
standing silent guard.
Then, as the travellers draw near,
they smile at their thoughts.
They see it's only, of course,
what it had to be.
And one of them inevitably
says to the other:
'That's all that's in it, it's only
an old manure bag.'

JO SLADE

Born in Berkhamsted, Hertfordshire, England in 1952 and educated at Limerick and National Colleges of Art, Jo Slade now works as a poet and painter in Limerick. A mother of two sons, her first collection, *In Fields I hear them Sing*, was published by Salmon in 1989. She has completed her second collection titled *The Vigilant One*.

When Our Heads Bend

When our heads bend,
We kiss.
We excite the deer
In her quiet wood,
We draw the hare
From his burrow.

Ballatuc

I was sixteen and my brother
Was fourteen when Ballatuc
Came to stay.

Our mother had died as
The snow fell
On our rusted fields

And magpies flew in pairs
From the stream
And nested in the garden.

I knew it wasn't good
I said it to Mike
'Those birds steal things'.

They took her body away
Her face was marble
And her hands like solid

Stones tucked beside her.
Ballatuc told me later
To forget those things

And I tried, but the mirror
Reminds me
I have hands like Mama's.

We finished with school
And started rising early
With the light,

The sun moved over the hedges
Until ragweed
By the ditches glowed,

We sat at the edge of the road
And talked as the night
Tied us in its soft, black toga.

Mike left us,
He went away with his mate,
I thought he'd write

Or come back when he'd found
Something. We never saw him again.
The stream makes his sound

When the rain swells it
And the small fish swim
At the bottom, where it's calm.

Ballatuc often kissed me
And when we shared the big bed
He went wild with his love,

He bit me, the way yard cats
Draw blood and then lick
Each other's wounds;

I could have coughed on him
A hail of sweet wine berries
And a sea of pebbles.

Ballatuc died in June.
I wouldn't let them
Take him away.

I stayed with him for days,
Then I washed his body
In the rain we kept to drink

And I put two stones
Into his eyes and I burned
Him by the stream.

EITHNE STRONG

Born in West Limerick in 1923, Eithne Strong was educated in Ennis and Trinity College, Dublin. Having reared her family Eithne studied for a degree. Jobs include working with the handicapped, freelance writing and teaching. She has given numerous readings at home and abroad and has had eleven books published with three new publications due in 1993, two volumes of poetry and a novel.

_____

The White Dress

I set behind me
all that happened
resurrected once again —
death and the grave twice already —
I felt the bind in my face
and set it free
my mouth laughed
and I put on a white dress.

I welcomed
the brightness
gathered up
a great armful
of primroses
their fragrance moved with me
all along the road.

The old black ghost of me
was lurking behind a tree
I turned fully towards it
my mouth wide wide
laughing.

When it returned
the following night
threatening suddenly
from a corner of the room
I gave it the same treatment.

Now at last
ah at last —
was not the dark long and bare? —
since I have on the white dress
the black ghost is powerless:
see me fleeting
to the bright field.

FRANCIS STUART

Francis Stuart was born in Australia in 1902, brought up in Co Antrim and educated in England. He taught for some years in Berlin University and now lives in Dublin. Though better known as a novelist, he has published the following poetry collections: *We Have Kept the Faith* (The Oak Leaf Press 1923), *New and Selected Poems: We Have Kept the Faith* (Raven Arts Press 1982), *Night Pilot* (Raven Arts Press 1988) and *We Have Kept the Faith: Poems 1918–1992* (Raven Arts Press 1992).

Berlin, 1944

Last night in that cafe
In a city in the middle of Europe,
Poised on the brink
Of the storm that was to be the end
To all that we know or think,
For a flash when I heard you say
A book's name: *Gone with the Wind*,
All was flowing, fleeting, slipping away
Until nothing was left, nothing was sure
But ourselves in the half-empty cafe,
We so rich, so frighteningly poor,
Your black eyes so hauntingly bright,
And only a moment left, an hour, a night.

Holiday

'And are you going to sit all day
Over that book?' I said,
'The car's outside.' That was last May,
I think, in Vallodolid.

There was a festival on
Downtown, and other things as well.
I wonder if we should have gone
Abroad at all. You said: 'Oh hell,

I don't want the car. I don't want you.
There's something better than all this,
A more exciting thing to do
Than gamble, drink and kiss.'

And then I saw beneath your hat
How your dark eyes suddenly shone
As you turned your face to me and shut
The gospel of St. John.

Night Pilot

The journey's getting longer every flight,
The black clouds blacker in their fringe of ice,
And in his ears the mariner's tolling bell
Of warning to the shuddering carapace
That earth looms up beneath the fragile shell.
The robot gadget landing blind and well
And he ever impatient to be gone
To the small house in which he is a guest
And whence lead half the runways of the globe,
But where he is without automaton
To ease the anguish of his inner probe,
Take on the risk and burden of his quest.

A Writer's Farewell

Bury me at Fatima Mansions
Between the wire and the wall
Within sound of the children's yelling
And their mothers' frantic call.

Encased beneath wet concrete
With nothing more to say,
My feet in ancient litter
And my head in Dublin clay.

As the washing waves above me
And the coal carts trundle by,
Unmarked and unremembered,
Safe at last I'd lie.

ACKNOWLEDGEMENTS

We are grateful to authors and publishers for permission to include poems from these sources.

Dermot Bolger from *Internal Exiles*, (Dolmen Press 1986); **Pat Boran** from *The Unwound Clock*, (Dedalus Press 1990); **Eva Bourke** from *Litany for the Pig*, (Salmon Publishing 1989); **Máire Bradshaw** from *The Box under the Bed An Anthology of Women's Writing* (Bradshaw Books 1986); **Rory Brennan** from *The Walking Wounded*, (Dedalus Press 1985); **Paddy Bushe** from *Poems with Amergin*, (Beaver Row Press 1989); **Catherine Byron** 'The Black and Tans Deliver her Cousin's Son' from *Settlements*, (Taxus Press 1985, with new edition due from Loxwood Stoneleigh 1993); and 'Shears' from *The Fat-Hen Field Hospital*, (Loxwood Stoneleigh 1993); **Kathleen Cain** from *Late Bloomers*, (Now it's Up to You Press 1987); **Siobhán Campbell** from the author; **Moya Cannon** from *Oar*, (Salmon Publishing 1990); **Seamus Cashman** 'The Mystery' and 'My Hero' from *Carnival*, (Monarch Line 1988), and 'A Final Fling' from the author; **Glenda Cimino** from *Cicada*, (Beaver Row Press 1988); **Michael Coady** 'Though There Are Torturers', The Jackdaws of Chapel Street' and 'Solo'from *Two for a Woman, Three for a Man*, (The Gallery Press 1980); other poems from *Oven Lane*, (The Gallery Press 1987); **Patrick Cotter** from *A Socialist's Dozen*, (The Three Spires Press 1990); **Tony Curtis** from *The Shifting of Stones*, (Beaver Row Press 1986); **Pádraig J. Daly** from *Dall'orlo Marino Del Mondo*, (Libreria Editrce Vaticana 1981); **John F. Deane** 'Questions', 'Miracle in Thomas Place', 'Missionary', 'Matins' and 'At a Grandmother's Grave' from *High Sacrifice*, (Dolmen Press 1981); 'Sacrament' from *Winter in Meath*, (Dedalus Press 1985); 'The Blue Toyota Van' from *Road with Cypress and Star*, (Dedalus Press 1988); **Greg Delanty** 'Out of the Ordinary' and 'Tie' from *Cast in the Fire*, (Dolmen, Press 1986), other poems from the author; **Theo Dorgan** from *The Ordinary House of Love*, (Salmon Publishing 1991); **Seán Dunne** from *Against the Storm*, (Dolmen Press 1985); **Gabriel Fitzmaurice** 'Portaireacht Bhéil', 'Garden', 'Epitaph' and 'Derelicts' from *Rainsong*, (Beaver Row Press 1984); 'In the Midst of Possibility' and 'Getting to Know You' from *Dancing Through*, (Beaver Row Press 1990); 'A Game of Forty-One' and 'The Hurt Bird' from *Road to the Horizon*, (Beaver Row Press 1987); **Patrick Galvin** from *Folk Tales for the General*, (Raven Arts Press 1989); **Anne Le Marquand Hartigan** 'Salt' from *Return Single*, (Beaver Row Press 1986); and from 'Winter the Man', the last section in *Now is a Moveable Feast*, (Salmon Publishing 1991); **Michael D. Higgins** from *The Betrayal*, (Salmon Publishing 1990); **Rita Ann Higgins** 'Poetry Doesn't Pay' and 'Mona' from *Goddess on the Mervue Bus*, (Salmon Publishing 1986); and 'The Did-You-Come-Yets of the Western World' from *Witch in the Bushes*, (Salmon Publishing 1988); **Fred Johnston** 'Letter to a Disciple' from *A Scarce Light*, (Beaver Row Press 1985); other poems from *Song at the End of the World*, (Salmon Publishing 1988); **Nan Joyce** from *Cyphers 21*, Summer 1984; **Anne Kennedy** from *Buck Mountain Poems*, (Salmon Publishing 1989); **Jerome Kiely** from *Yesterdays of the Heart*, (Dedalus Press 1989); **Jessie Lendennie** from *Daughter*, (Salmon Publishing 1988); **John Liddy** from *The Angling Cot*, (Beaver Row Press 1991); **Joan Mc Breen** from *The Wind beyond the Wall*, (Story Line Press 1990); **Steve Mac Donogh** from *By Dingle Bay and Blasket Sound*, (Brandon Book Publishers 1991); **Máire Mhac an Tsaoi** from *An Cion go dtí Seo*, (Sáirséal Ó Marcaigh); Translations 'Quatrains of Mary Hogan' and 'The Hero's Sleep' by the author and 'Christmas Eve' by Gabriel Fitzmaurice all from *An Crann faoi Bhláth/The Flowering Tree*, (Wolfhound Press 1991); **Tomás Mac Síomóin** from *Codarsnai*, (Clodhanna Teoranta) and the author's translation from *An Crann faoi Bhláth/The Flowering Tree*, (Wolfhound Press 1991); **Caitlín Maude** Irish poems from *Caitlin Maude Danta*, (Coiscéim 1984) and translations by Gabriel Fitzmaurice from *An Crann faoi Bhláth/The Flowering Tree*, (Wolfhound Press 1991); **Paula Meehan** from *The Man who was marked by Winter*, (The Gallery Press 1991); **Tom Morgan** 'Haven' and 'The Aspidistra' from *Nan of the Falls Rd.*, *Curfew*, (Beaver Row Press 1990); and 'Easter in the West' from *The Rat Diviner*, (Beaver Row Press 1987); **Gerry Murphy** from *A Cartoon History of the Spanish Civil War*, (Three Spires Press 1991); **Paul Murray** from *Rites and Meditations*, (Dolmen Press 1982); **Áine Ní Ghlinn** Irish poems from *An Chéim Bhriste*, (Coiscéim 1984); and translations by Gabriel Fitzmaurice from *An Crann faoi Bhláth/The Flowering Tree*, (Wolfhound Press 1991); **Pat O'Brien** from *A Book of Genesis*, (Dedalus

INDEX

Press 1988); **Julie O'Callaghan** from *Edible Anecdotes*, (Dolmen Press 1983); **Clairr O'Connor** from *When you need them*, (Salmon Publishing 1989); **Ulick O'Connor** 'Easter Week 1986' from *All Things Counter,* (Dedalus Press 1986); other poems from *One is Animate*, (Beaver Row Press 1990); **Hugh O'Donnell** from *Roman Pines at Berkeley*, (Salmon Publishing 1990); **Mary O'Donnell** from *Reading the Sunflowers in September*, (Salmon Publishing 1990); **Bernard O'Donoghue** 'Bulmer' from *Poaching Rights*, (The Gallery Press 1987); other poems from *The Weakness*, (Chatto and Windus 1991); **Ciaran O'Driscoll** 'Man with Macaw' from *Gog and Magog*, (Salmon Publishing 1987); other poems from *The Poet and his Shadow*, (Dedalus Press 1990); **Dennis O'Driscoll** 'Someone' and 'Flat Life' from *Kist*, (Dolmen Press 1982); other poems from *Hidden Extras*, (Anvil Books/Dedalus Press 1987); **Gréagóir Ó Dúill** 'Athbhliain', 'Geimhreadh' from the author, and 'Don Chonstábla Taca Michael Williams' from *Blaoscoileán*, (Coiscéim 1988); translations 'New Year' and 'Winter' by Aodán MacPóilin and 'For Reserve Constable Michael Williams' by Pádraig MacFhearghusa; **Mary O'Malley** from *A Consideration of Silk*, (Salmon Publishing 1990); **Cathal Ó Searcaigh** 'Bó Bhradach', from *An Bealach 'na Bhaile Homecoming, Selected Poems of Cathal O Searcaigh*, (Clo Iar-Chonnachta 1993); Translation 'A Braddy Cow' by Gabriel Fitzmaurice; **Micheal O'Siadhail** 'In a New York Shoe Shop', 'Visionary', 'Stranger', 'Questing' and 'Nest' reprinted by permission of Bloodaxe Books Ltd from *Hail! Madam Jazz: New and Selected Poems by Micheal O'Siadhail* (Bloodaxe Books 1992). 'Nead', 'Nugent' and the author's own translation 'Nugent' from *An Crann faoi Bhláth/The Flowering Tree*, (Wolfhound Press 1991); **Pádraig Ó Snodaigh** as *Ó Pharnell go Queenie*, (Coiscéim 1991) and translation 'From Parnell to Queenie by Gabriel Fitzmaurice; **Derry O'Sullivan** 'Marbhghin 1943 Glaoch ar Liombó' and 'Foighne' from *Ca bhfuil do Iúdás*, (Coiscéim 1987); translation by the author, 'Patience' from *The King's English*, (First Impressions Paris 1987) and translation by Michael Davitt, 'Stillborn 1943 A Call to Limbo' from *Translation* vol XXIII, New York, Fall 1989; **Gabriel Rosenstock** 'Tóraíocht' and 'Teilifís' from *Om*, (An Clócomhar 1983); translations 'The Search', 'Billie Holiday' and 'Television' by Gabriel Fitzmaurice from *An Crann faoi Bhláth/The Flowering Tree*, (Wolfhound Press 1991); 'Billie Holiday' from *Migmars* (Ababuna 1985); 'anois' and 'sliabh' from *Méaram*, (An Clócomhar 1981); translations 'now' and 'mountain' by Gabriel Fitzmaurice; **Deirdre Shanahan** from *Legal Tender*, (Enitharmon Press, UK, 1988); **Joe Sheerin** from *A Crack in the Ice*, (Dolmen Press 1985); **Knute Skinner** from *Learning to Spell Zucchini*, (Salmon Publishing 1988); **Jo Slade** from *In Fields I Hear them Sing*, (Salmon Publishing 1989); **Eithne Strong** from *Let Live*, (Salmon Publishing 1990); **Francis Stuart** from *Night Pilot*, (Raven Arts Press 1988).

288